JUMBLE® Gymnastics

Henri Arnold,
Bob Lee,
Mike Argirion,
Jeff Knurek, &
David L. Hoyt

TRIUMPH
BOOKS

This book is available in quantity at special discounts
for your group or organization.

For further information, contact:

Triumph Books LLC
814 North Franklin Street
Chicago, Illinois 60610
Phone: (312) 337-0747
www.triumphbooks.com

Printed in U.S.A.

ISBN: 978-1-62937-306-5

Design by Sue Knopf

CONTENTS

JUMBLE®

Gymnastics

Classic Puzzles

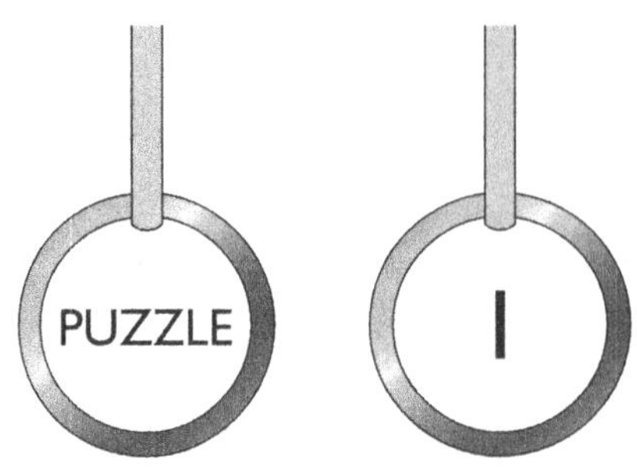
PUZZLE
1

JUMBLE®

Unscramble these four Jumbles, one letter to each square, to form four ordinary words.

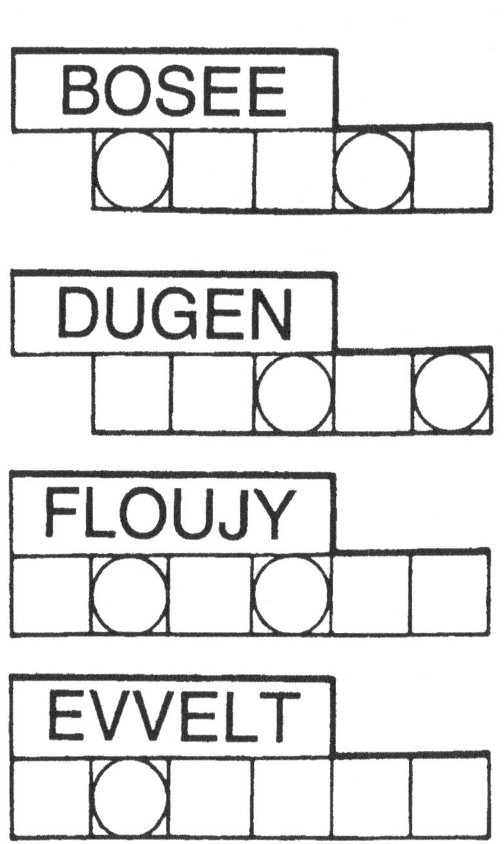
BOSEE
DUGEN
FLOUJY
EVVELT

It all looks so good
WHAT A CAFETERIA OFFERS.

Now arrange the circled letters to form the surprise answer, as suggested by the above cartoon.

Print answer here

PUZZLE
2

JUMBLE®

Unscramble these four Jumbles, one letter to each square, to form four ordinary words.

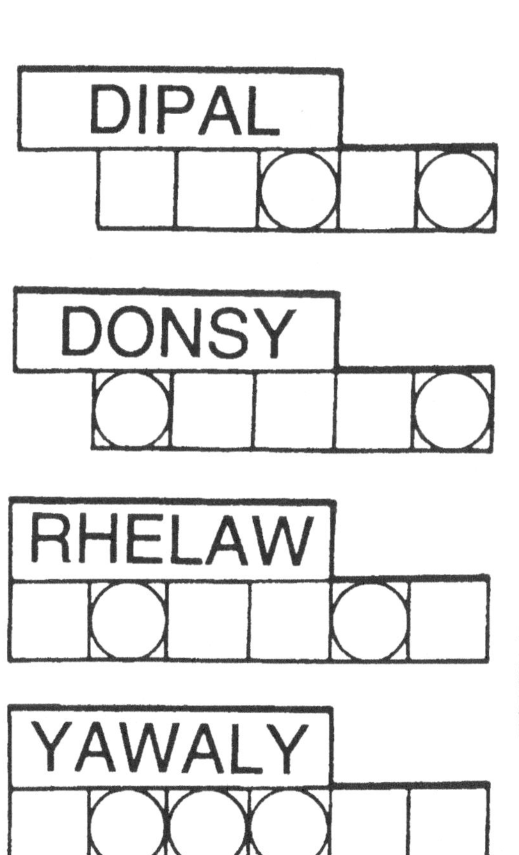
DIPAL
DONSY
RHELAW
YAWALY

All or nothing--
How about it?
WHAT THEY CONSIDERED THE CARD SHARK'S SUGGESTION.

Now arrange the circled letters to form the surprise answer, as suggested by the above cartoon.

Print answer here A  

PUZZLE
3

JUMBLE®

Unscramble these four Jumbles, one letter to each square, to form four ordinary words.

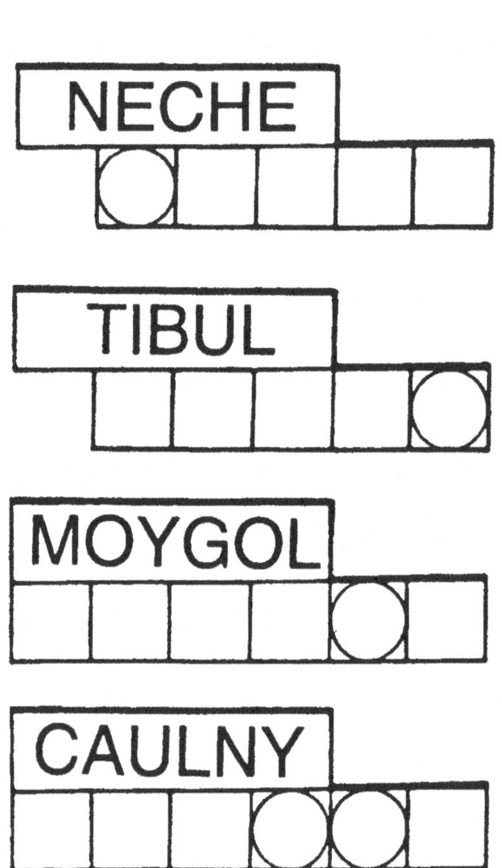
NECHE
TIBUL
MOYGOL
CAULNY

Do you have a light?
WHAT SHE WAS LOOKING FOR AT THE SINGLES DANCE.

Now arrange the circled letters to form the surprise answer, as suggested by the above cartoon.

Print answer here A 

PUZZLE
4

JUMBLE®

Unscramble these four Jumbles, one letter to each square, to form four ordinary words.

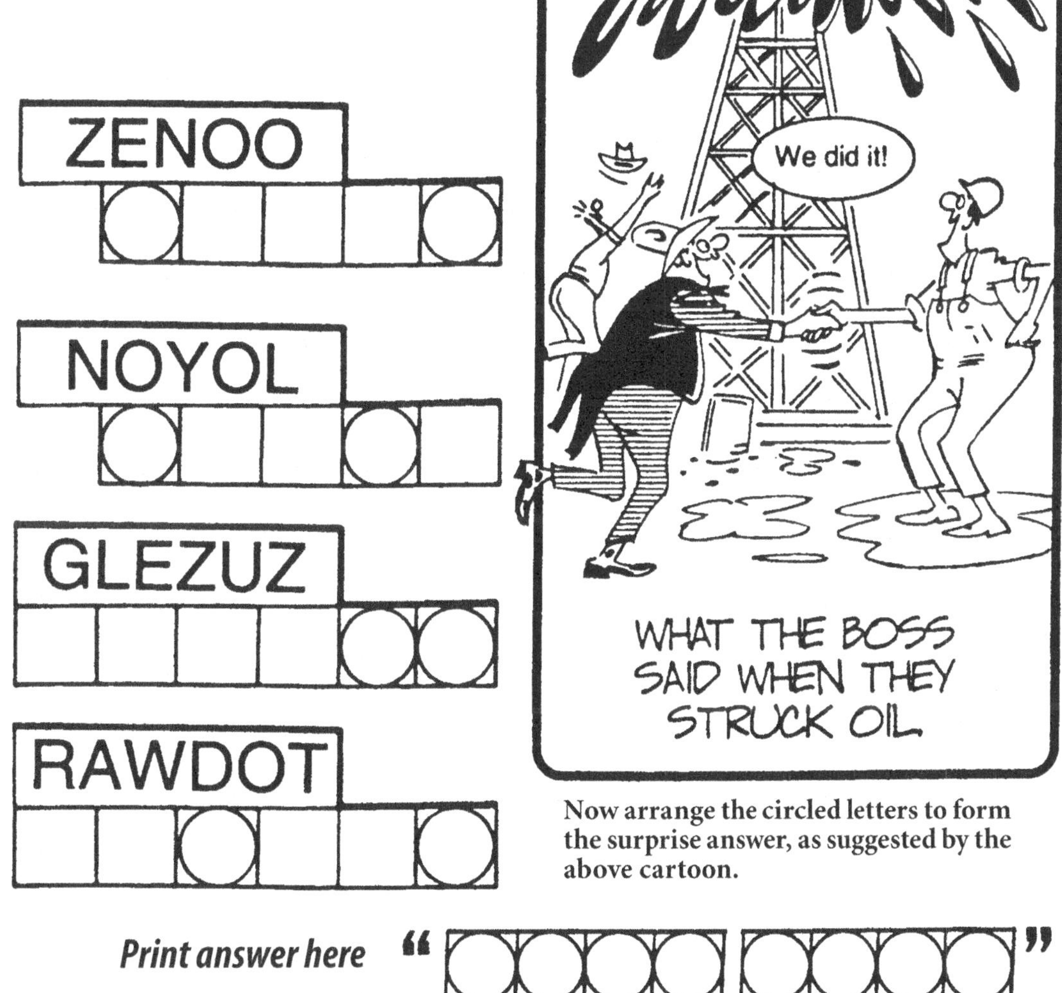
ZENOO
NOYOL
GLEZUZ
RAWDOT
We did it!
WHAT THE BOSS SAID WHEN THEY STRUCK OIL

Now arrange the circled letters to form the surprise answer, as suggested by the above cartoon.

Print answer here " "

PUZZLE
5

JUMBLE®

Unscramble these four Jumbles, one letter to each square, to form four ordinary words.

SCEHS

SULEO

ECPPIT

YITAGE

He went up there

After him, men!

PURSUING THE CHURCH THIEF RESULTED IN THIS.

Now arrange the circled letters to form the surprise answer, as suggested by the above cartoon.

Print answer here A

PUZZLE
6

JUMBLE®

Unscramble these four Jumbles, one letter to each square, to form four ordinary words.

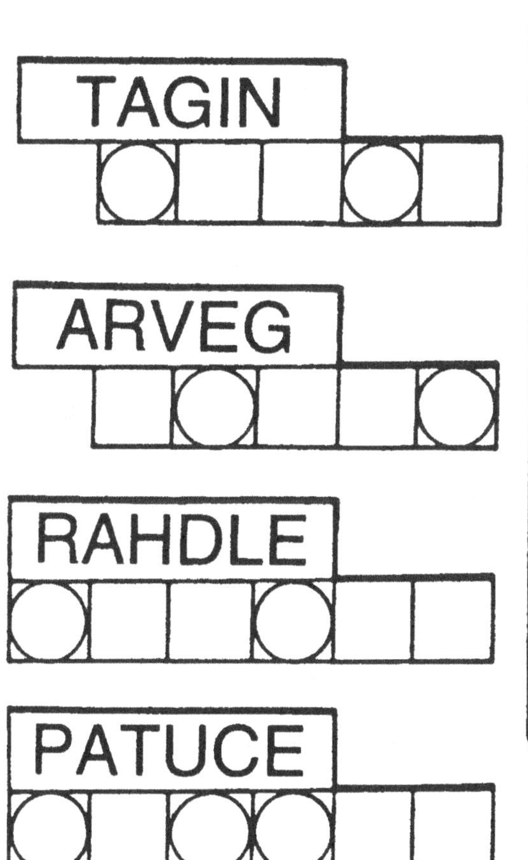
TAGIN
ARVEG
RAHDLE
PATUCE

On second thought, I think I'll substitute a different painting
WHAT THE ENGLISH DECORATOR HAD.

Now arrange the circled letters to form the surprise answer, as suggested by the above cartoon.

Print answer here A ◯◯◯◯◯◯ OF '◯◯◯

PUZZLE
7

JUMBLE®

Unscramble these four Jumbles, one letter to each square, to form four ordinary words.

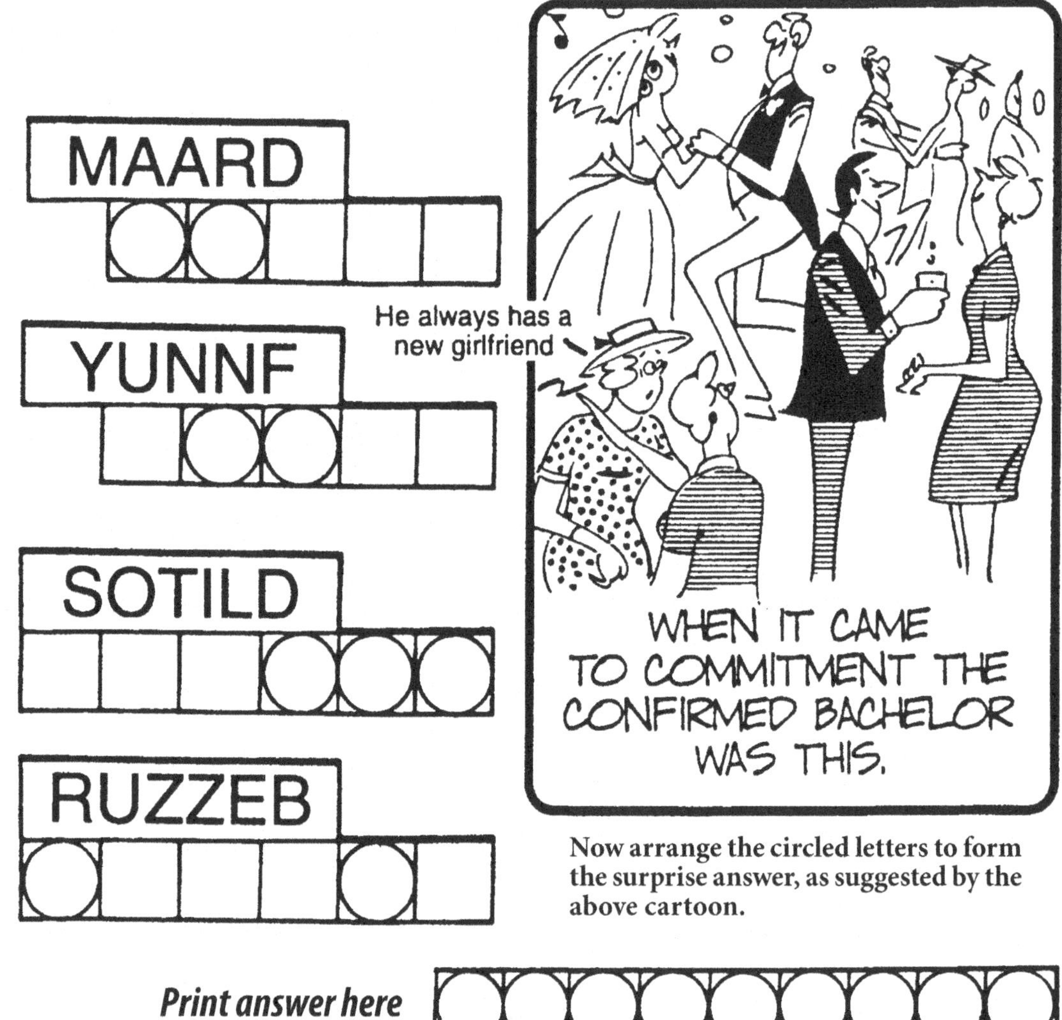
MAARD
YUNNF
SOTILD
RUZZEB
He always has a new girlfriend
WHEN IT CAME TO COMMITMENT THE CONFIRMED BACHELOR WAS THIS.

Now arrange the circled letters to form the surprise answer, as suggested by the above cartoon.

Print answer here

PUZZLE
8

JUMBLE®

Unscramble these four Jumbles, one letter to each square, to form four ordinary words.

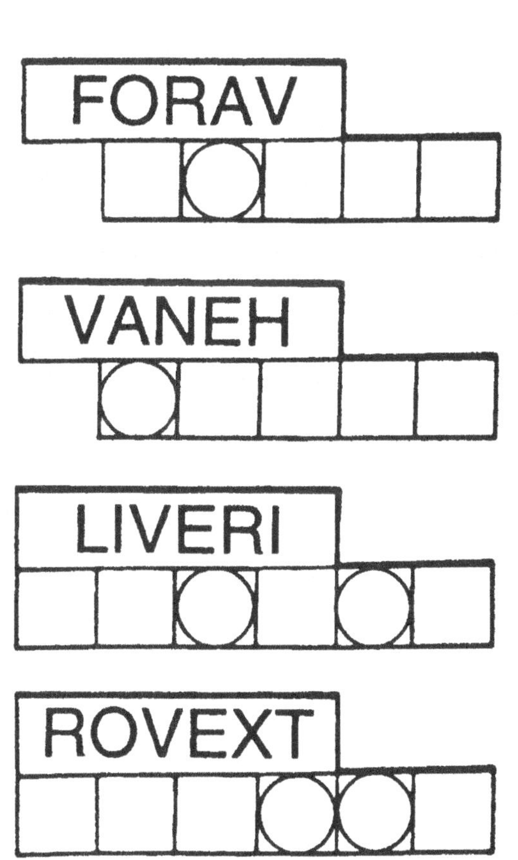
FORAV
VANEH
LIVERI
ROVEXT

WHEN THE WASHING MACHINE BROKE IT LEFT MOM---

Now arrange the circled letters to form the surprise answer, as suggested by the above cartoon.

Print answer here IN A

PUZZLE
9

JUMBLE®

Unscramble these four Jumbles, one letter to each square, to form four ordinary words.

SMUNI
ZAUER
DORRAM
URREBB
CORPORATE BLACK MOODS CAN BE CAUSED BY THIS.

Now arrange the circled letters to form the surprise answer, as suggested by the above cartoon.

Print answer here

PUZZLE
10

JUMBLE®

Unscramble these four Jumbles, one letter to each square, to form four ordinary words.

GITUL
SOMEO
MINTIG
JURNIY
Bad day for everyone
WHAT LAWYERS OFTEN FACE IN A COURTROOM.
Now arrange the circled letters to form the surprise answer, as suggested by the above cartoon.
Print answer here

PUZZLE
11

JUMBLE®

Unscramble these four Jumbles, one letter to each square, to form four ordinary words.

DUNOB

GINVY

WENITH

FIELDE

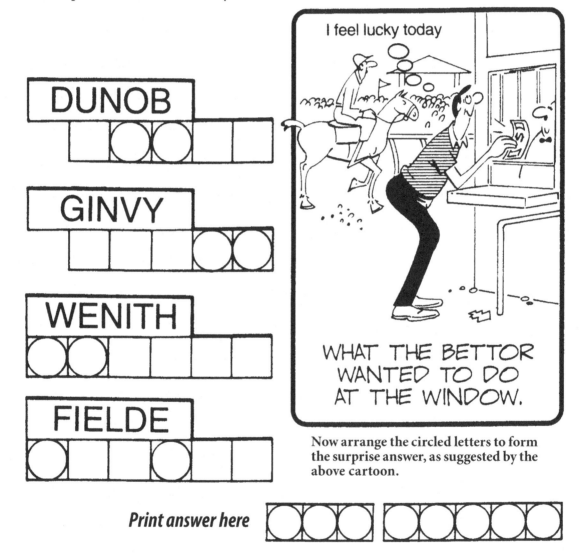

I feel lucky today

WHAT THE BETTOR WANTED TO DO AT THE WINDOW.

Now arrange the circled letters to form the surprise answer, as suggested by the above cartoon.

Print answer here

PUZZLE
12

JUMBLE®

Unscramble these four Jumbles, one letter to each square, to form four ordinary words.

FITAH

AKARP

DOLSUN

JONNIE

Got anything for a blister?
WHAT THE RUNNER CALLED THE INITIAL STOP IN THE MARATHON.

Now arrange the circled letters to form the surprise answer, as suggested by the above cartoon.

Print answer here “ ”

PUZZLE
13

JUMBLE®

Unscramble these four Jumbles, one letter to each square, to form four ordinary words.

ECASE
SYRTT
NILUKE
DISMOW
Who's been reading my paper?
BREAKFAST JAM ON THE MORNING PAPER CAN BECOME THIS.
Print answer here
A

Now arrange the circled letters to form the surprise answer, as suggested by the above cartoon.

PUZZLE
14

JUMBLE®

Unscramble these four Jumbles, one letter to each square, to form four ordinary words.

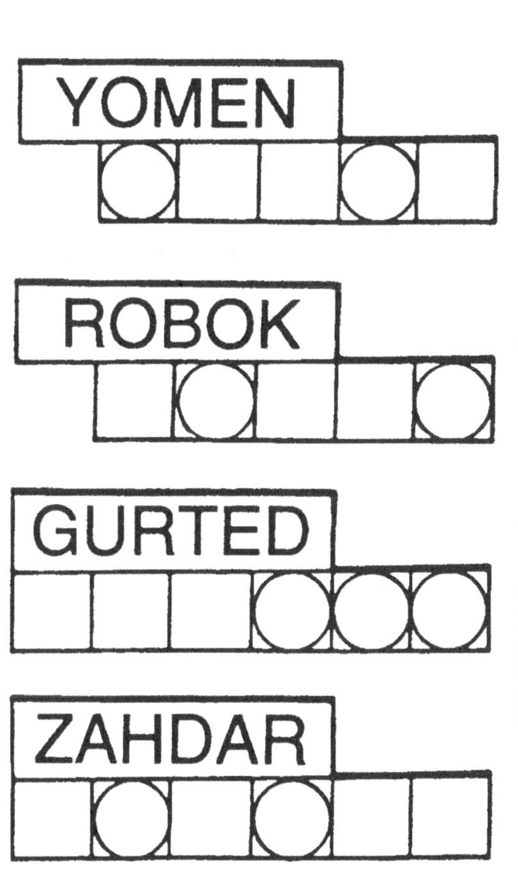
YOMEN
ROBOK
GURTED
ZAHDAR

Nice job
He'll go far
SUCCESSFUL ROAD BUILDERS DO THIS.

Now arrange the circled letters to form the surprise answer, as suggested by the above cartoon.

Print answer here

THE

PUZZLE
15

JUMBLE®

Unscramble these four Jumbles, one letter to each square, to form four ordinary words.

MEVON
BARRO
LADDEY
BRUBUS
Relax...next train's two hours away
WHERE THE HOBOS LIKED TO REST.

Now arrange the circled letters to form the surprise answer, as suggested by the above cartoon.

Print answer here ON A “ ”

PUZZLE
16

JUMBLE®

Unscramble these four Jumbles, one letter to each square, to form four ordinary words.

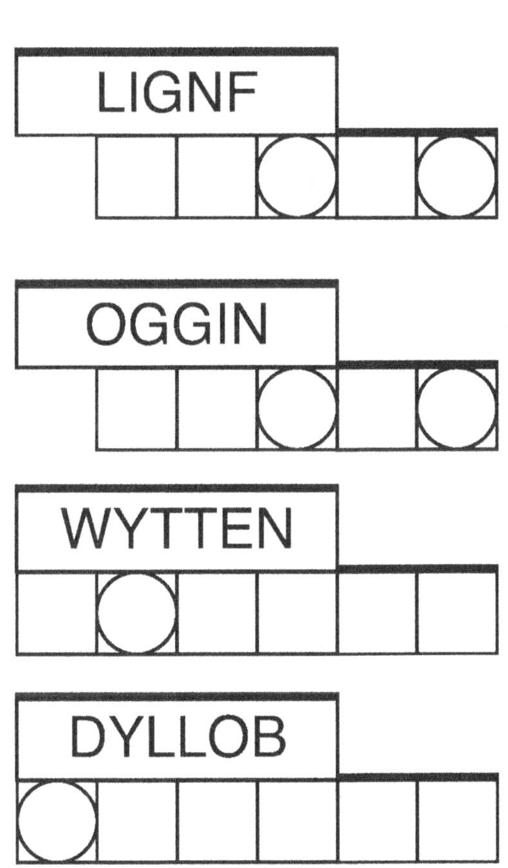
LIGNF
OGGIN
WYTTEN
DYLLOB

I've decided to expand our factory since my designs have taken off.
Hi, boss!
THE OWNER OF THE TOUPEE COMPANY WAS A ---

Now arrange the circled letters to form the surprise answer, as suggested by the above cartoon.

Print answer here

PUZZLE
17

JUMBLE®

Unscramble these four Jumbles, one letter to each square, to form four ordinary words.

KNLAF

AABET

CAFEDA

RITPUN

This Vulcan character is a strange fellow.
Have you talked to him yet?
This is a most peculiar hand gesture.
LEONARD NIMOY'S CAREER REALLY TOOK OFF AS A RESULT OF HIM BEING ---

Now arrange the circled letters to form the surprise answer, as suggested by the above cartoon.

Print answer here "◯◯◯◯◯-◯◯◯◯"

PUZZLE
18

JUMBLE®

Unscramble these four Jumbles, one letter to each square, to form four ordinary words.

RIUVS
CADEY
RUTFOH
LEHTAH

What's up?
Not much. I thought you were going to telling me a joke.
TAKE
HE DIDN'T GET THE JOKE ABOUT THE CEILING BECAUSE IT WAS ---

Now arrange the circled letters to form the surprise answer, as suggested by the above cartoon.

Print answer here

PUZZLE
19

JUMBLE®

Unscramble these four Jumbles, one letter to each square, to form four ordinary words.

INOON

HATSS

PECULO

UCORAG

Yep. That's what I have.
I've got 105.
105
105

WHEN THEY COUNTED THE PRISONERS, THE RESULT WAS A ---

Now arrange the circled letters to form the surprise answer, as suggested by the above cartoon.

Print answer here "___-______"

PUZZLE
20

JUMBLE®

Unscramble these four Jumbles, one letter to each square, to form four ordinary words.

OFCER
RUNPS
AMOOTT
NILMEG
I've sold more shrimp than you can count. I think I'll buy another boat.
That's amazing, Forrest. You should open a restaurant.
Jenny
FORREST GUMP'S SHRIMP BUSINESS RESULTED IN ---

Now arrange the circled letters to form the surprise answer, as suggested by the above cartoon.

Print answer here

PUZZLE
21

JUMBLE®

Unscramble these four Jumbles, one letter to each square, to form four ordinary words.

NITEG
SIYPT
NATMED
FLARMO
I'll tell you what. You've got some moves.
You're not too bad yourself. You almost had me a bunch of times.
BUG OFF
I ♥ JUMBLE
THE INSECT WAS NO LONGER BUGGING HIM, AND WAS QUICKLY BECOMING HIS ---

Now arrange the circled letters to form the surprise answer, as suggested by the above cartoon.

Print answer here " ◯◯◯◯ " ◯◯◯◯◯◯

PUZZLE
22

JUMBLE®

Unscramble these four Jumbles, one letter to each square, to form four ordinary words.

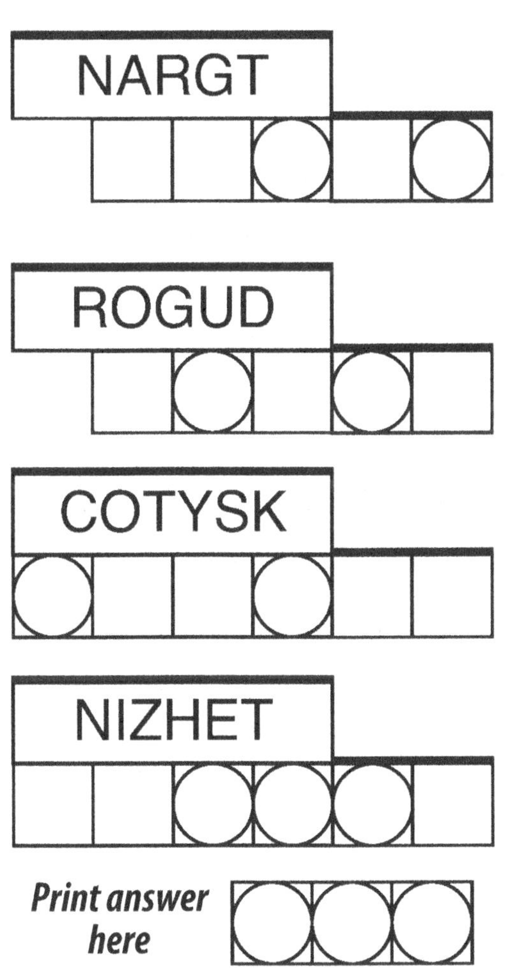
NARGT
ROGUD
COTYSK
NIZHET

Wanna Picasso for $500?
That's not a Picasso!
2-Way Wrist Radio
Tracy, here! I found our grifter.
T.R.I.B.
Pulitzer Winner
Jumble cartoonist wins
HE ARRESTED THE PAINTER BECAUSE HE WAS A ---

Now arrange the circled letters to form the surprise answer, as suggested by the above cartoon.

Print answer here

PUZZLE
23

JUMBLE®

Unscramble these four Jumbles, one letter to each square, to form four ordinary words.

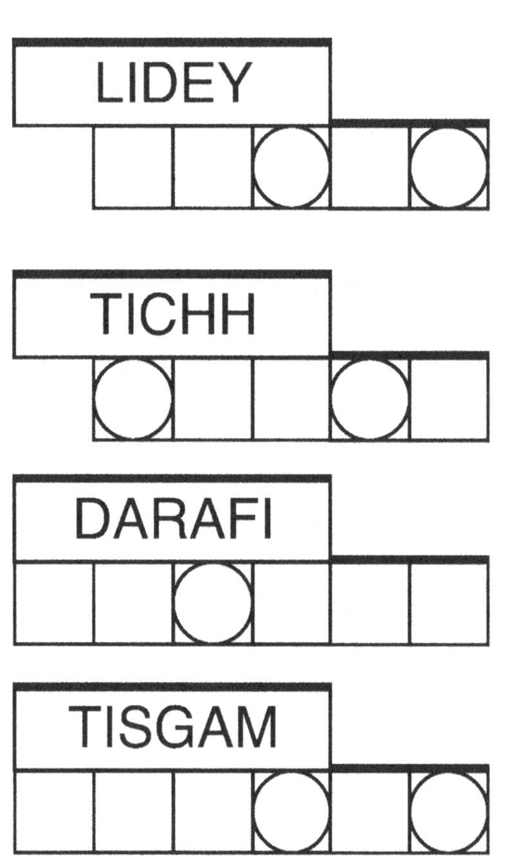
LIDEY
TICHH
DARAFI
TISGAM

You're looking at grand theft, Sparky.
I'll book him, Tracy.
You can't prove anything.
AFTER THE THIEF WAS CAUGHT STEALING THE BATTERIES, HE WAS ---

Now arrange the circled letters to form the surprise answer, as suggested by the above cartoon.

Print answer here

PUZZLE
24

JUMBLE®

Unscramble these four Jumbles, one letter to each square, to form four ordinary words.

FUWAL
KTELN
KNARCY
GAADEN

You're not getting me, Tracy!
B.O., come out! We've got you surrounded.
AFTER FLEEING INTO THE LAUNDROMAT, THE SUSPECT HAD NO CHANCE OF A ---

Now arrange the circled letters to form the surprise answer, as suggested by the above cartoon.

Print answer here

PUZZLE
25

JUMBLE®

Unscramble these four Jumbles, one letter to each square, to form four ordinary words.

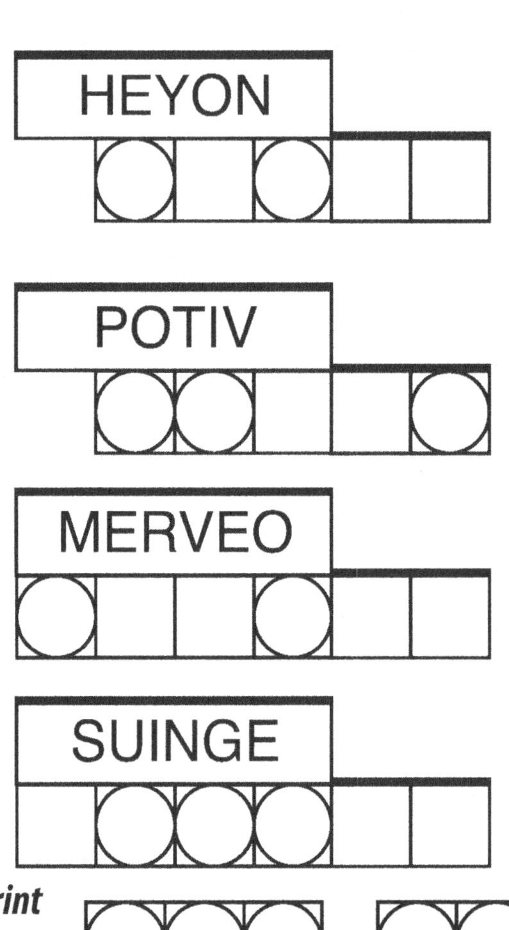
HEYON
POTIV
MERVEO
SUINGE

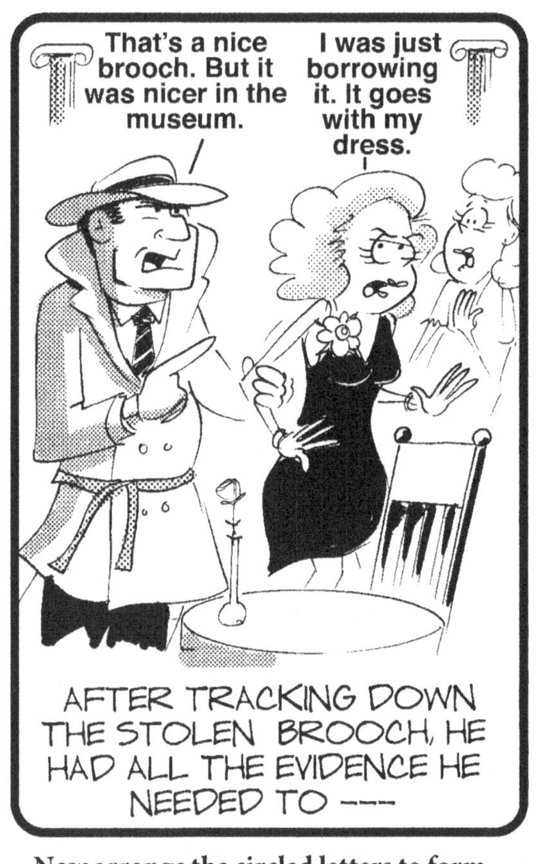
That's a nice brooch. But it was nicer in the museum.
I was just borrowing it. It goes with my dress.
AFTER TRACKING DOWN THE STOLEN BROOCH, HE HAD ALL THE EVIDENCE HE NEEDED TO ---

Now arrange the circled letters to form the surprise answer, as suggested by the above cartoon.

Print answer here

JUMBLE®

Gymnastics

Daily Puzzles

PUZZLE
26

JUMBLE®

Unscramble these four Jumbles, one letter to each square, to form four ordinary words.

CCILK

RAFEM

CISYLK

THIRGB

There is no escape. Watch and learn.
REBELS 10 267
EMPIRE 9 238
You'll need to force three in a row to win.
Going down are you.
THE REBEL BOWLING TEAM WAS LEADING, BUT PLAYERS WORRIED THE EMPIRE'S TEAM MIGHT---

Now arrange the circled letters to form the surprise answer, as suggested by the above cartoon.

Print answer here

PUZZLE
27

JUMBLE®

Unscramble these four Jumbles, one letter to each square, to form four ordinary words.

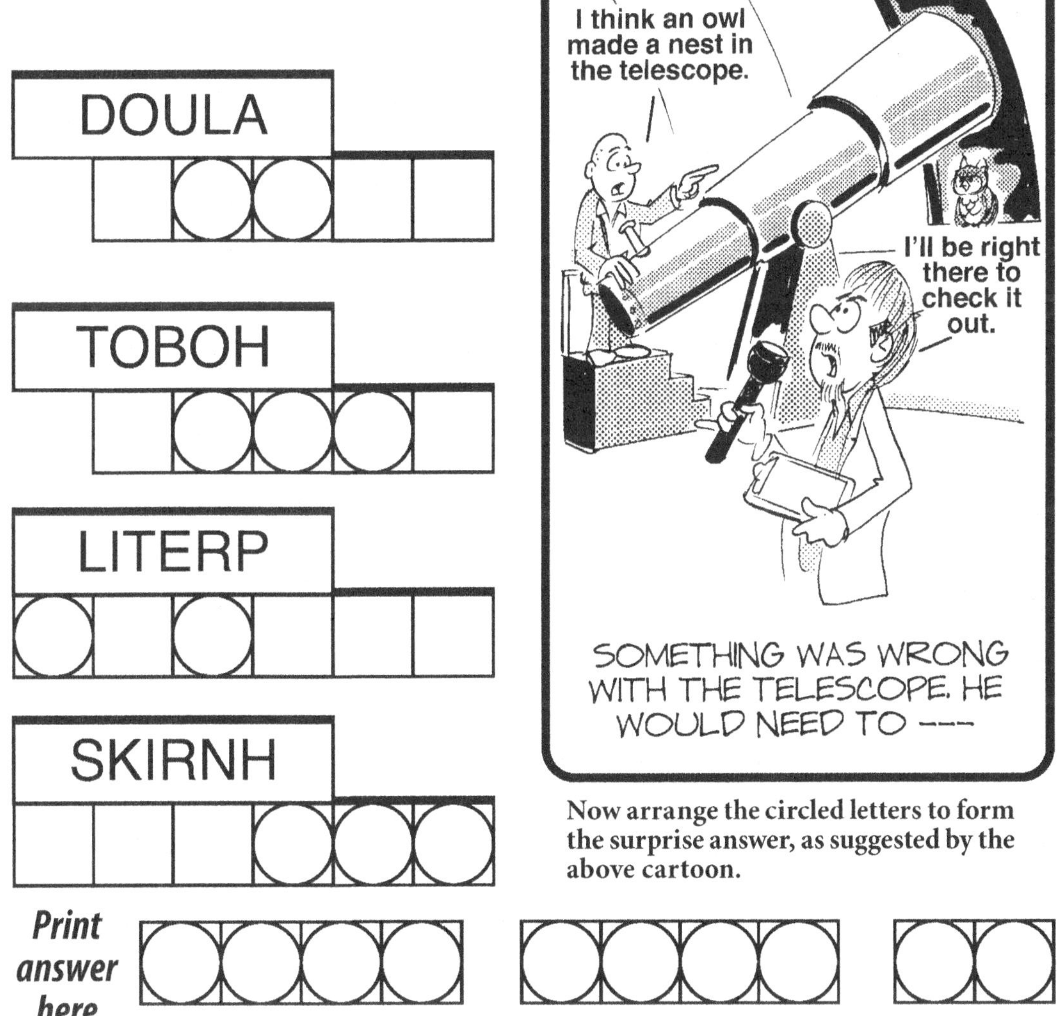
DOULA
TOBOH
LITERP
SKIRNH
I think an owl made a nest in the telescope.
I'll be right there to check it out.
SOMETHING WAS WRONG WITH THE TELESCOPE. HE WOULD NEED TO ---
Print answer here

Now arrange the circled letters to form the surprise answer, as suggested by the above cartoon.

PUZZLE
28

JUMBLE®

Unscramble these four Jumbles, one letter to each square, to form four ordinary words.

AVTUL
KRELC
SOLNES
NICADD
You're going to love this!
Foie gras, sir.
THE FOOD WAS PRETTY GOOD AT THE SKUNK RESTAURANT, BUT THE ---
Now arrange the circled letters to form the surprise answer, as suggested by the above cartoon.
Print answer here

PUZZLE
29

JUMBLE®

Unscramble these four Jumbles, one letter to each square, to form four ordinary words.

KLISY
YEHAV
DISGIN
LAFNEL
I think one more coat will do it.
SHINE
SHE WOULD APPLY COATS OF VARNISH UNTIL THE TABLE WAS ---

Now arrange the circled letters to form the surprise answer, as suggested by the above cartoon.

Print answer here

PUZZLE
30

JUMBLE®

Unscramble these four Jumbles, one letter to each square, to form four ordinary words.

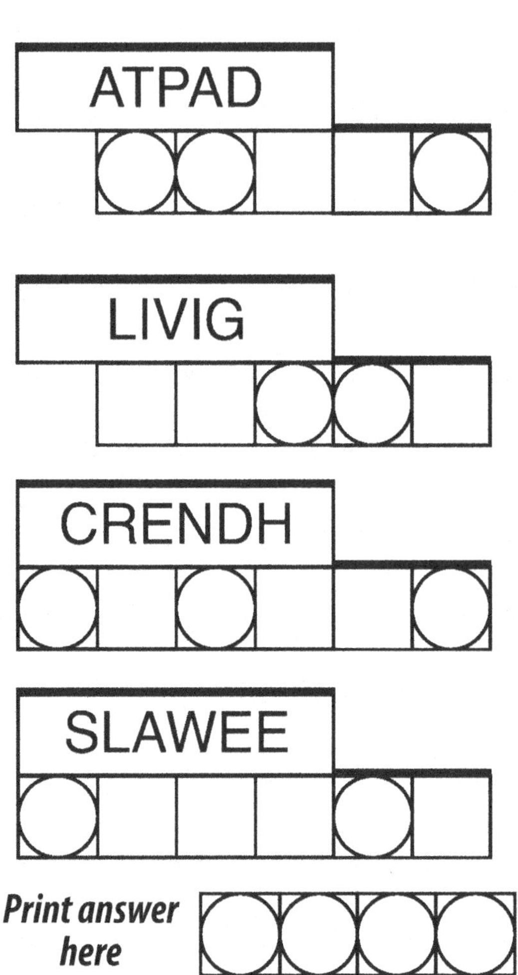
ATPAD
LIVIG
CRENDH
SLAWEE

I thought you'd be lighter.
HS
THE ZOMBIE BRIDE WAS HARD TO CARRY OVER THE THRESHOLD BECAUSE SHE WAS ---

Now arrange the circled letters to form the surprise answer, as suggested by the above cartoon.

Print answer here

PUZZLE
31

JUMBLE®

Unscramble these four Jumbles, one letter to each square, to form four ordinary words.

NEVMO
LLAST
HITCEN
SUTNUJ
The room's decor was dated. Your breakfast was inedible. Have you ever owned a B&B before?
You don't have many friends, do you?
THE GUEST'S RUDE COMMENTS ABOUT THE LODGING ESTABLISHMENT WERE ---

Now arrange the circled letters to form the surprise answer, as suggested by the above cartoon.

Print answer here "◯◯◯-◯◯◯◯◯"

PUZZLE
32

JUMBLE®

Unscramble these four Jumbles, one letter to each square, to form four ordinary words.

KALNB
TEABA
ROCCSH
CIKELP
I thought we were going to diet together. You have got to stop eating!
It's the last slice.
IN ORDER TO LOSE WEIGHT, THE OVEREATER WOULD NEED TO ---

Now arrange the circled letters to form the surprise answer, as suggested by the above cartoon.

Print answer here

PUZZLE
33

JUMBLE®

Unscramble these four Jumbles, one letter to each square, to form four ordinary words.

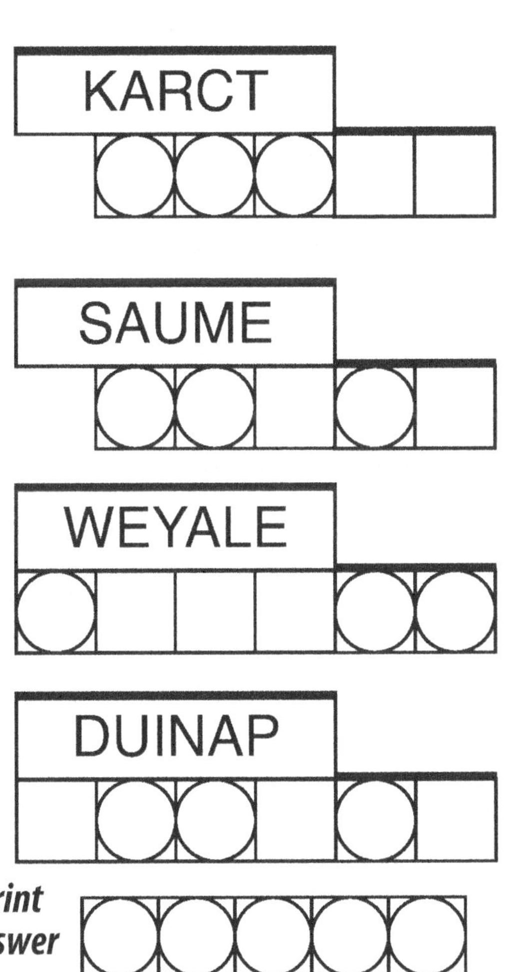
KARCT
SAUME
WEYALE
DUINAP

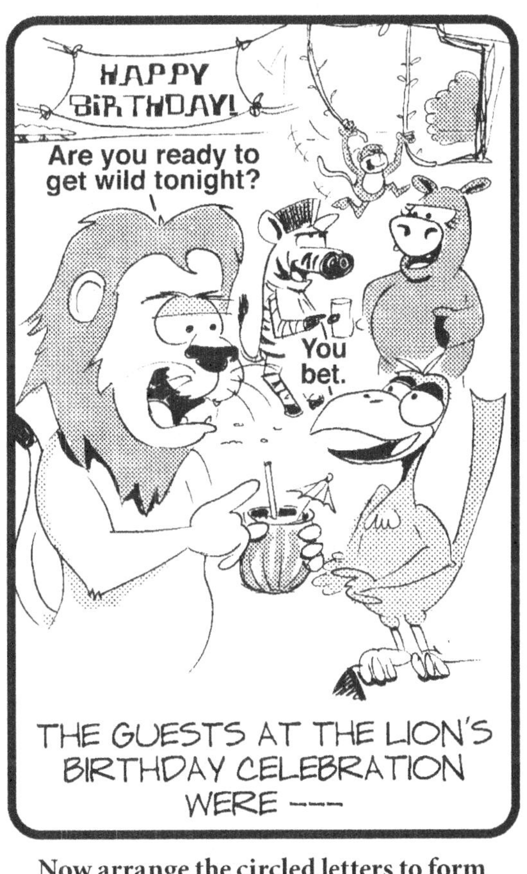
HAPPY BIRTHDAY!
Are you ready to get wild tonight?
You bet.
THE GUESTS AT THE LION'S BIRTHDAY CELEBRATION WERE ---

Now arrange the circled letters to form the surprise answer, as suggested by the above cartoon.

Print answer here

PUZZLE
34

JUMBLE®

Unscramble these four Jumbles, one letter to each square, to form four ordinary words.

ROWNS
CREPH
MUTUNA
SOBBRA
Your boys are much better than mine. Who's the better golfer?
They're both great.
WHEN IT CAME TO HIS TWIN BOYS, THERE WAS NO ---
Now arrange the circled letters to form the surprise answer, as suggested by the above cartoon.
Print answer here
" - - "

PUZZLE
35

JUMBLE®

Unscramble these four Jumbles, one letter to each square, to form four ordinary words.

SERFH

KOLCC

FIXLUN

TADCEH

Look! I don't want what you're selling. Leave us alone!
Not again!
You tell them, Dad.
HE THOUGHT THE TELEMARKETER'S INTERRUPTION WAS ---

Now arrange the circled letters to form the surprise answer, as suggested by the above cartoon.

Print answer here

PUZZLE
36

JUMBLE®

Unscramble these four Jumbles, one letter to each square, to form four ordinary words.

ADAHE

FORLO

VATREN

LILHRS

All right. Five bucks apiece.
Here you go.
Here's mine.
That will be $15, guys.
JUMBLE CAB
WHEN THEY SPLIT THE COST OF THE TAXI RIDE, EVERYONE PAID HIS ---

Now arrange the circled letters to form the surprise answer, as suggested by the above cartoon.

Print answer here " ◯◯◯◯ " ◯◯◯◯◯

PUZZLE
37

JUMBLE®

Unscramble these four Jumbles, one letter to each square, to form four ordinary words.

GEBIE

MUCPH

PEGION

RUPUSE

Now we have a tree for every one of the kids.
I'm glad they're having a sale.
Buy One Get One 50% OFF!

THEIR TRIP TO THE CHRISTMAS TREE FARM TURNED INTO A ---

Now arrange the circled letters to form the surprise answer, as suggested by the above cartoon.

Print answer here " "

PUZZLE
38

JUMBLE®

Unscramble these four Jumbles, one letter to each square, to form four ordinary words.

TENVE
YABSS
SIMTIF
BALIVE
We've got a seat open.
I don't think that's a good idea.
Do you want to play?
It's just a friendly game.
DECLINING THEIR OFFER TO JOIN THE POKER GAME WOULD BE HIS ---

Now arrange the circled letters to form the surprise answer, as suggested by the above cartoon.

Print answer here

PUZZLE
39

JUMBLE®

Unscramble these four Jumbles, one letter to each square, to form four ordinary words.

CIMMI
SHALS
CEDIVE
HOIPAB
Who wants to go out and fix the gyroscope?
I do! I'm getting claustrophobic.
THE ASTRONAUT VOLUNTEERED FOR THE SPACEWALK BECAUSE SHE WANTED ---
Print answer here

Now arrange the circled letters to form the surprise answer, as suggested by the above cartoon.

PUZZLE
40

JUMBLE®

Unscramble these four Jumbles, one letter to each square, to form four ordinary words.

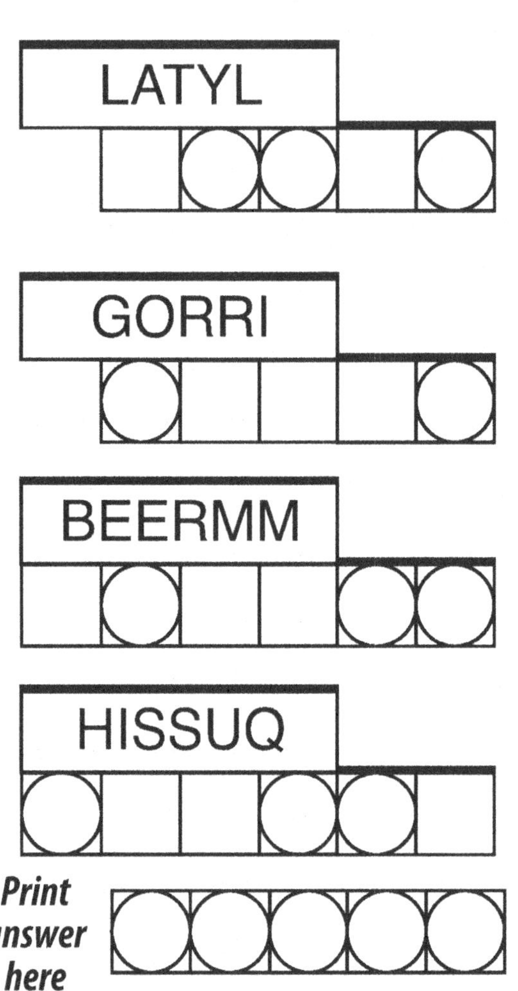
LATYL
GORRI
BEERMM
HISSUQ

We need to get a better view.
Let's head to the top of the hill.
THEY CLIMBED THE HILL TO SEE THE SUN COME UP BECAUSE THEY WERE ---

Now arrange the circled letters to form the surprise answer, as suggested by the above cartoon.

Print answer here

PUZZLE
41

JUMBLE®

Unscramble these four Jumbles, one letter to each square, to form four ordinary words.

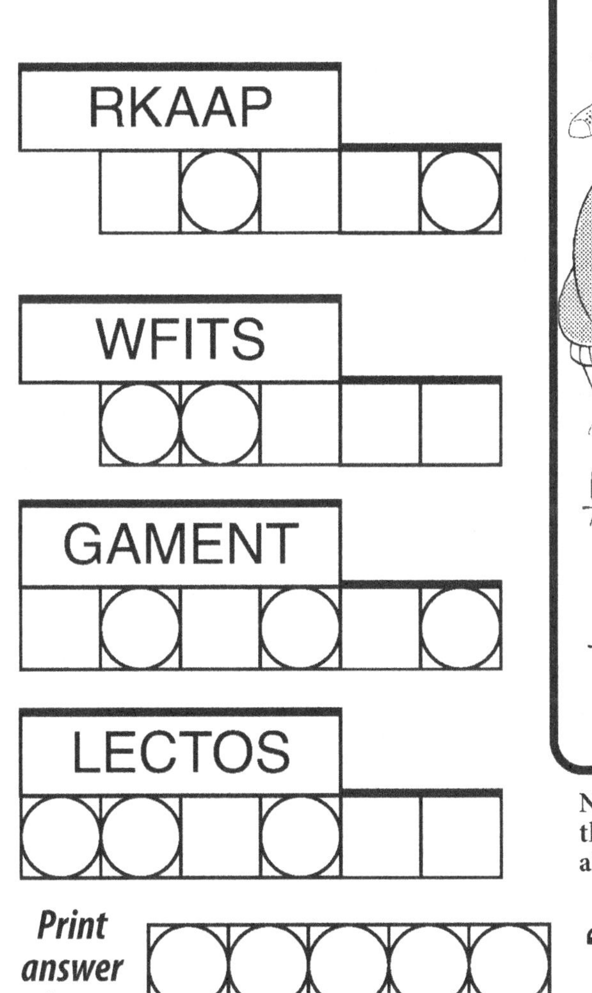
RKAAP
WFITS
GAMENT
LECTOS

Let's not forget the boots.
Don't be naughty, Tootie.
THE CHRISTMAS COSTUME BROUGHT OUT THEIR CAT'S ---

Now arrange the circled letters to form the surprise answer, as suggested by the above cartoon.

Print answer here

PUZZLE
42

JUMBLE®

Unscramble these four Jumbles, one letter to each square, to form four ordinary words.

RIPPM

CAWMA

YADWES

LENYOL

Greetings, friends! Come on in! Enjoy my latest invention.
Thank you for inviting us, Mr. Franklin.
Goodness! It's so pleasant in here.
AFTER HE INVENTED THE FRANKLIN STOVE, BEN WAS ABLE TO GIVE PEOPLE A ---

Now arrange the circled letters to form the surprise answer, as suggested by the above cartoon.

Print answer here

PUZZLE
43

JUMBLE®

Unscramble these four Jumbles, one letter to each square, to form four ordinary words.

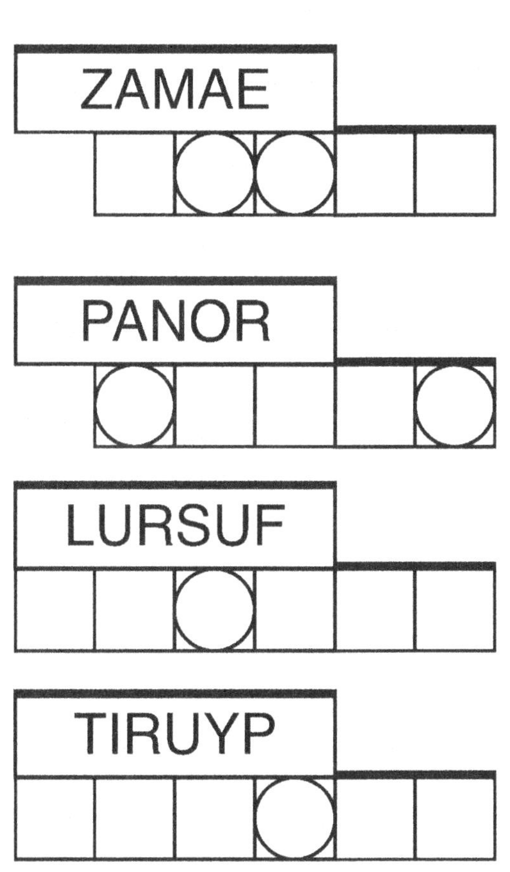
ZAMAE
PANOR
LURSUF
TIRUYP

She's the only elephant at the zoo.
I can tell she's an Asian elephant by her ears.
WHAT CAN YOU FIND IN "MANILA" THAT YOU CAN'T FIND IN "TOKYO"?

Now arrange the circled letters to form the surprise answer, as suggested by the above cartoon.

Print answer here

PUZZLE
44

JUMBLE®

Unscramble these four Jumbles, one letter to each square, to form four ordinary words.

LEKAN
GLINC
RAPHIS
XEDOUT
How about if we call it Britain?
I love it!
Jolly good!
WHEN THEY DECIDED TO NAME THEIR ISLAND "BRITAIN," EVERYONE THOUGHT IT WAS ---

Now arrange the circled letters to form the surprise answer, as suggested by the above cartoon.

Print answer here A

PUZZLE
45

JUMBLE®

Unscramble these four Jumbles, one letter to each square, to form four ordinary words.

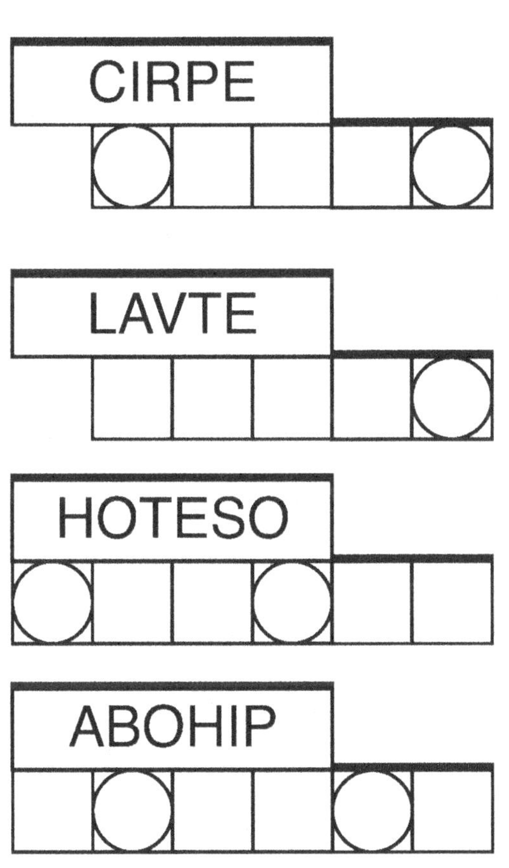
CIRPE
LAVTE
HOTESO
ABOHIP

Great game today!
Excuse me.
You, too!
SOMETIMES, CHANGING IN THE LOCKER ROOM IS ---

Now arrange the circled letters to form the surprise answer, as suggested by the above cartoon.

PUZZLE
46

JUMBLE®

Unscramble these four Jumbles, one letter to each square, to form four ordinary words.

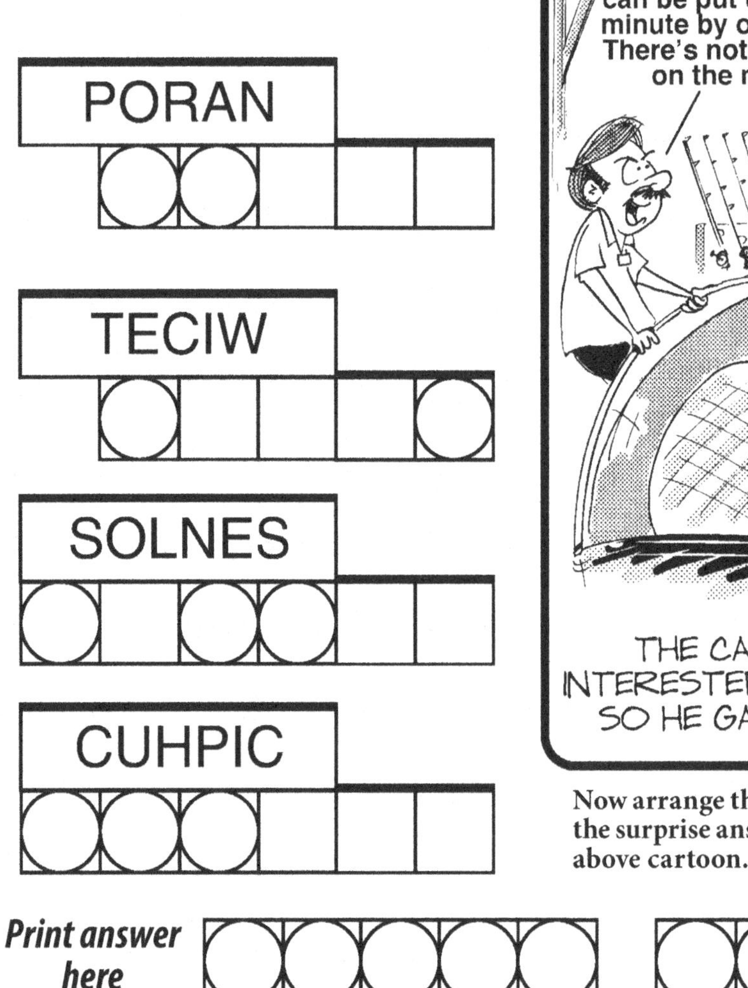

PORAN
TECIW
SOLNES
CUHPIC

As you can see, it can be put up in just a minute by one person. There's nothing better on the market!
Wow!
THE CAMPERS WERE INTERESTED IN A NEW TENT, SO HE GAVE THEM A ---

Now arrange the circled letters to form the surprise answer, as suggested by the above cartoon.

Print answer here

PUZZLE
47

JUMBLE®

Unscramble these four Jumbles, one letter to each square, to form four ordinary words.

RIHEK

KLECR

TYPSOT

EYELAW

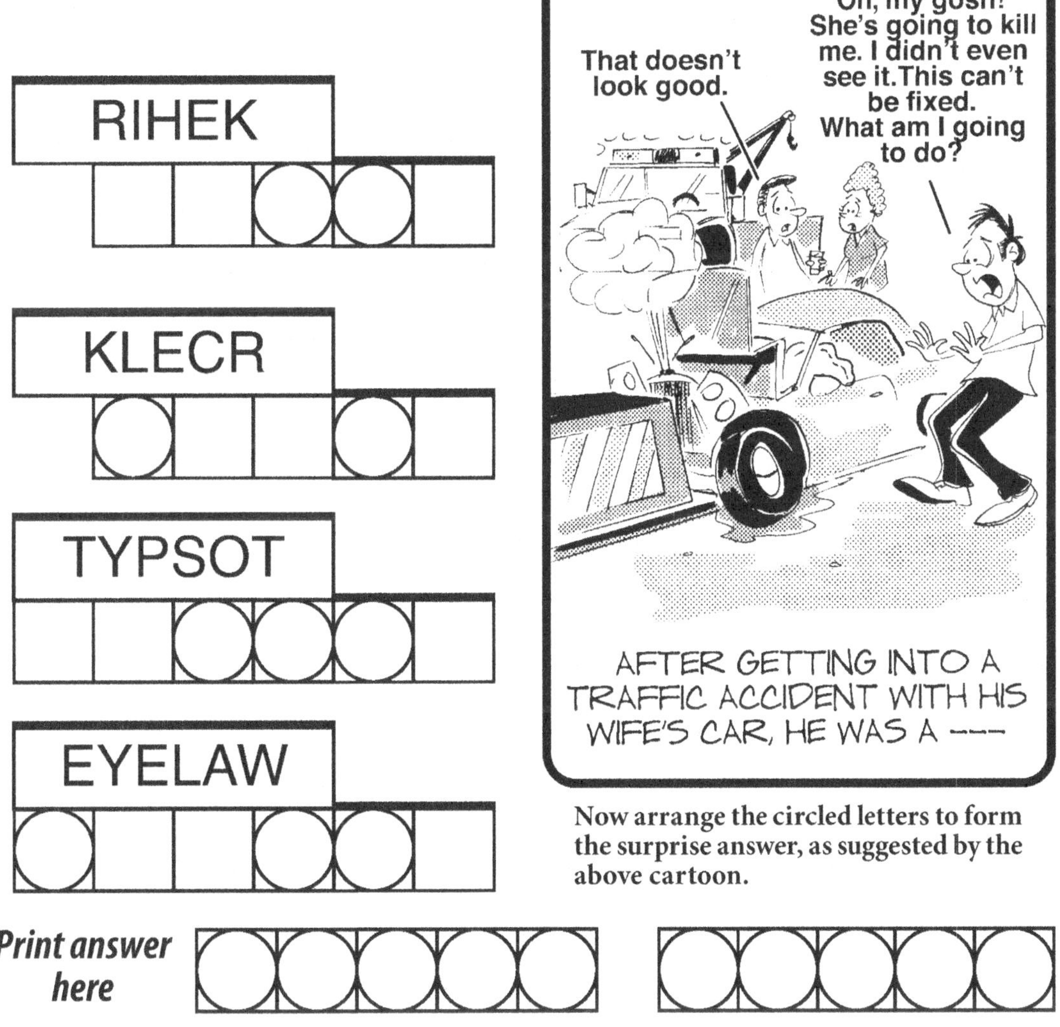
That doesn't look good.
Oh, my gosh! She's going to kill me. I didn't even see it.This can't be fixed. What am I going to do?
AFTER GETTING INTO A TRAFFIC ACCIDENT WITH HIS WIFE'S CAR, HE WAS A ---

Now arrange the circled letters to form the surprise answer, as suggested by the above cartoon.

Print answer here

PUZZLE
48

JUMBLE®

Unscramble these four Jumbles, one letter to each square, to form four ordinary words.

TUYOH

PIEML

CUBSAA

CEDDEA

C'mon! Do you want a piece of pepperoni or cheese? I don't have all day.
ORDER HERE!
Uh, yes. I'll take one of each.
He's rude.
THE PIZZA PARLOR'S APPROACH TO GETTING CUSTOMERS TO MAKE A PURCHASE WAS ---

Now arrange the circled letters to form the surprise answer, as suggested by the above cartoon.

Print answer here "◯◯◯" ◯◯◯ ◯◯◯◯◯

PUZZLE
49

JUMBLE®

Unscramble these four Jumbles, one letter to each square, to form four ordinary words.

NAGIT
TOBOH
LABIVE
BUARUN
THE DOCUMENTARY ABOUT THE CONSTRUCTION OF THE EIFFEL TOWER WAS ---

Now arrange the circled letters to form the surprise answer, as suggested by the above cartoon.

Print answer here

PUZZLE
50

JUMBLE®

Unscramble these four Jumbles, one letter to each square, to form four ordinary words.

RULBT

CHERP

VONCIE

THOLCB

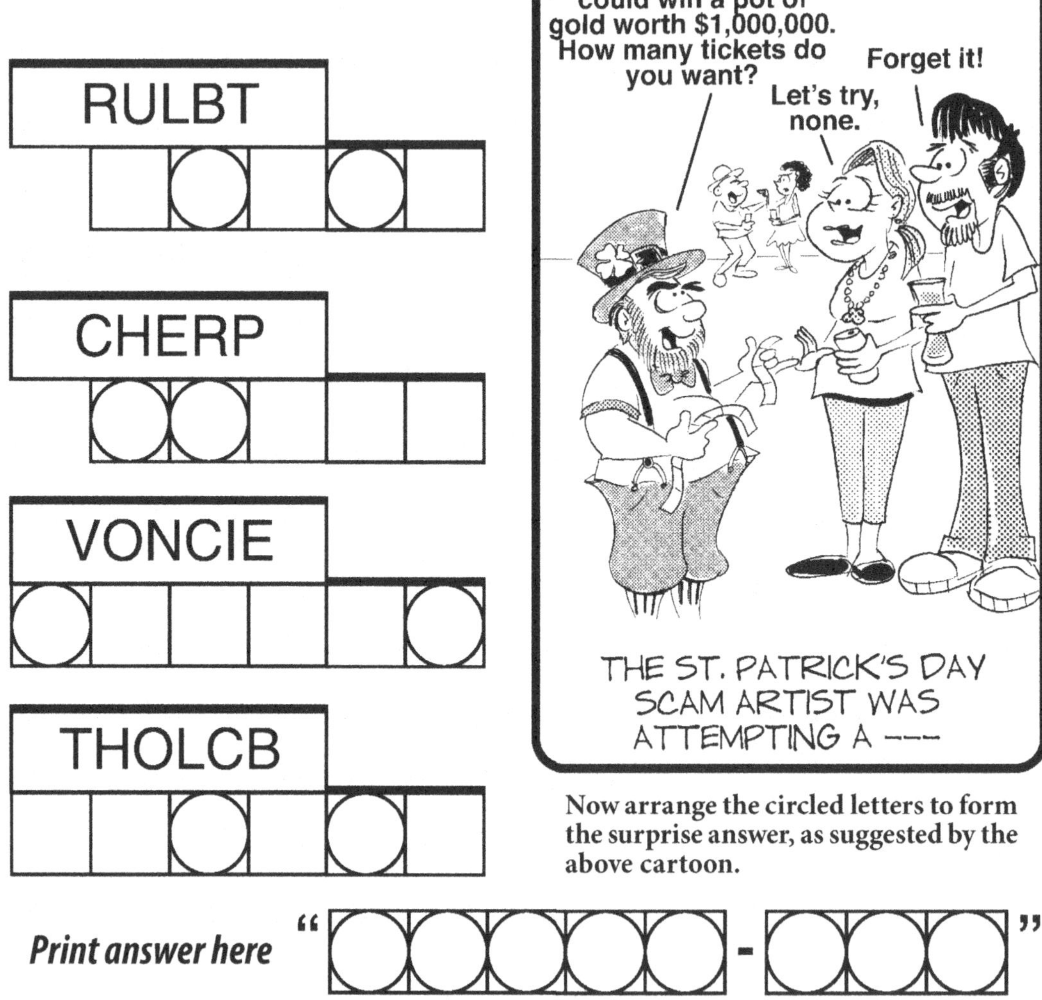
For just $20, you could win a pot of gold worth $1,000,000. How many tickets do you want?
Let's try, none.
Forget it!
THE ST. PATRICK'S DAY SCAM ARTIST WAS ATTEMPTING A ---

Now arrange the circled letters to form the surprise answer, as suggested by the above cartoon.

Print answer here " - "

PUZZLE
51

JUMBLE®

Unscramble these four Jumbles, one letter to each square, to form four ordinary words.

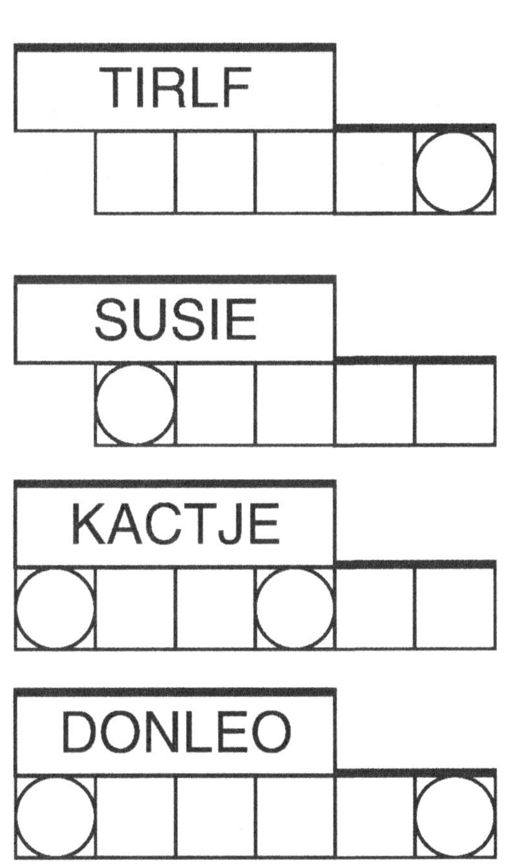
TIRLF
SUSIE
KACTJE
DONLEO

That was quick. Can I read it?
I just finished printing my report.
TO PRINT OUT THE PAGE WITH THE BOEING 747 ON IT, HE USED ----

Now arrange the circled letters to form the surprise answer, as suggested by the above cartoon.

Print answer here AN  

PUZZLE
52

JUMBLE®

Unscramble these four Jumbles, one letter to each square, to form four ordinary words.

ECINE

DARUF

DILNAS

GEEERM

Stop! You'll get eaten alive!
There's nothing to worry about. I just need to cool off.
Sir, don't! It's not safe.
HE DIDN'T THINK HE WOULD BE EATEN BY A CROCODILE, BUT HE WAS ---

Now arrange the circled letters to form the surprise answer, as suggested by the above cartoon.

Print answer here ◯◯ "◯◯-◯◯◯◯"

PUZZLE
53

JUMBLE
Unscramble these four Jumbles, one letter to each square, to form four ordinary words.
BOIRT
MOVEN
CESNIK
LUGRAF

Why has the price gone up since our first meeting?
Well, we have to keep up with inflation.
THE CEMETERY RAISED ITS BURIAL FEES AND BLAMED IT ON THE ---

Now arrange the circled letters to form the surprise answer, as suggested by the above cartoon.

Print answer here

PUZZLE
54

JUMBLE®
Unscramble these four Jumbles, one letter to each square, to form four ordinary words.
ASORE
FONET
TIMSAG
SANDIU
Hey. Here's the calendar I posed for in college.
That's you? That was a long time ago.
BILL'S COLLEGE STUFF
THE FORMER MALE MODEL'S CALENDAR PHOTOS WERE ---
Now arrange the circled letters to form the surprise answer, as suggested by the above cartoon.
Print answer here

PUZZLE
55

JUMBLE®

Unscramble these four Jumbles, one letter to each square, to form four ordinary words.

DOTSO

FETHT

THAWCS

ECIAPE

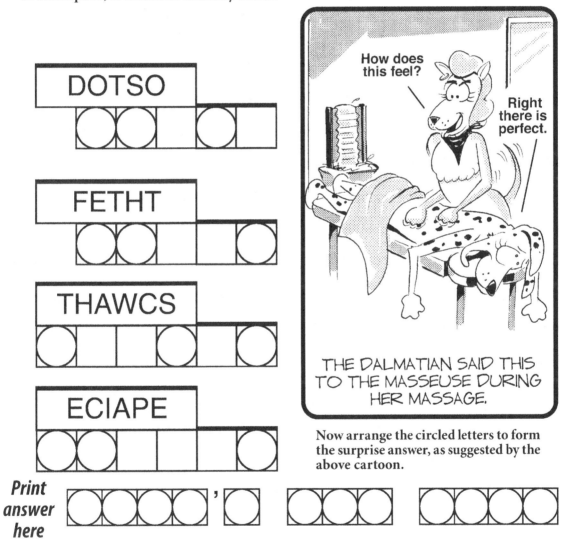

How does this feel?

Right there is perfect.

THE DALMATIAN SAID THIS TO THE MASSEUSE DURING HER MASSAGE.

Now arrange the circled letters to form the surprise answer, as suggested by the above cartoon.

Print answer here

◯◯◯◯'◯ ◯◯◯ ◯◯◯◯

PUZZLE
56

JUMBLE®

Unscramble these four Jumbles, one letter to each square, to form four ordinary words.

YICIL

ALMEY

HERTIE

SLAQUL

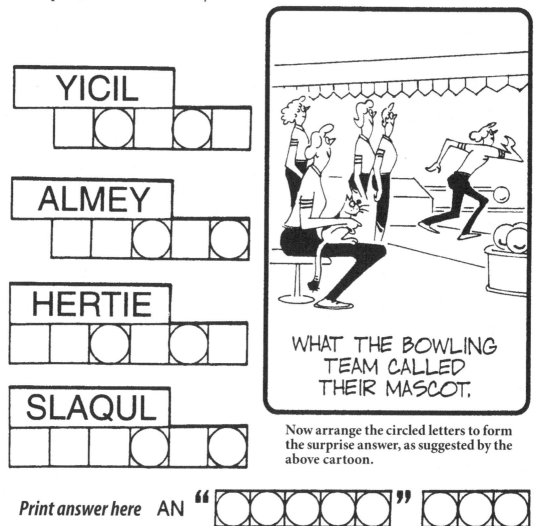

WHAT THE BOWLING TEAM CALLED THEIR MASCOT.

Now arrange the circled letters to form the surprise answer, as suggested by the above cartoon.

Print answer here AN " "

PUZZLE
57

JUMBLE®

Unscramble these four Jumbles, one letter to each square, to form four ordinary words.

NIROY
PYMUB
AHNRAG
SWILEY
We never made calls to all these people
$
WHAT SHE KEPT GETTING ON HER PHONE BILL.
Print answer here

Now arrange the circled letters to form the surprise answer, as suggested by the above cartoon.

PUZZLE
58

JUMBLE®

Unscramble these four Jumbles, one letter to each square, to form four ordinary words.

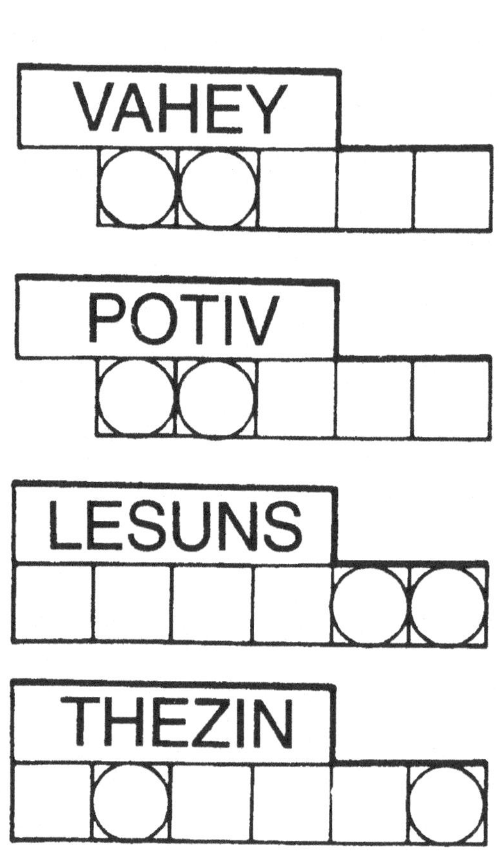
VAHEY
POTIV
LESUNS
THEZIN

Where did they all go?
HOW THE HERDER FELT WHEN HE LOST HIS FLOCK.

Now arrange the circled letters to form the surprise answer, as suggested by the above cartoon.

Print answer here

PUZZLE
59

JUMBLE®

Unscramble these four Jumbles, one letter to each square, to form four ordinary words.

COTIN

UVESA

NIFTIE

SLYGUN

My favorite--you remembered

WHY HE BOUGHT HER PERFUME.

Now arrange the circled letters to form the surprise answer, as suggested by the above cartoon.

Print answer here HE WAS [ ]-[ ]

PUZZLE
60

JUMBLE®

Unscramble these four Jumbles, one letter to each square, to form four ordinary words.

LUKKS
BREEM
LIBART
NECCAT
WHAT THE TEAM CALLED THEIR ANNUAL DANCE.

Now arrange the circled letters to form the surprise answer, as suggested by the above cartoon.

Print answer here THE ◯◯◯◯◯◯ "◯◯◯◯◯"

PUZZLE
61

JUMBLE®

Unscramble these four Jumbles, one letter to each square, to form four ordinary words.

ZISEE
SYSUF
FLUGEN
VERREE
No more!
WHAT OVERLOADED TRASH COLLECTORS DO.

Now arrange the circled letters to form the surprise answer, as suggested by the above cartoon.

Print answer here

PUZZLE
62

JUMBLE®

Unscramble these four Jumbles, one letter to each square, to form four ordinary words.

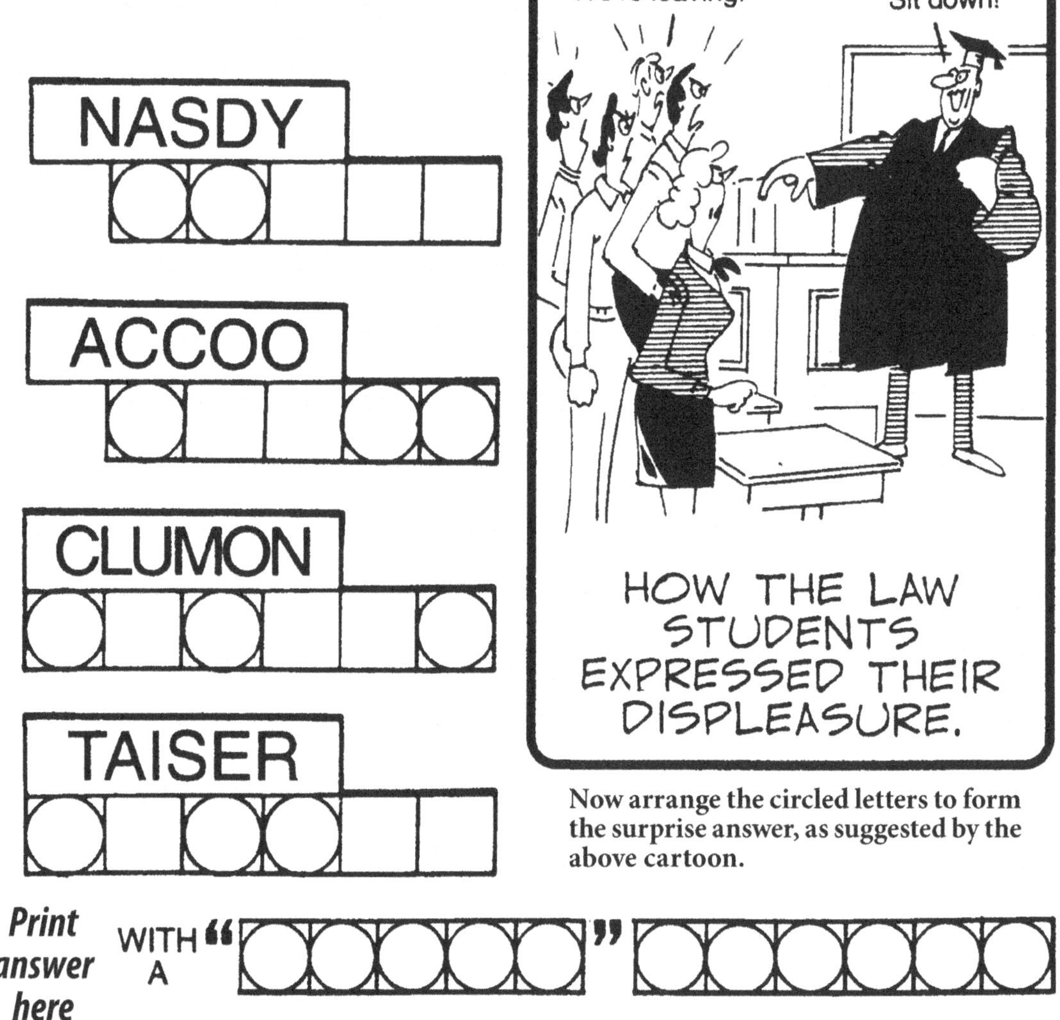
NASDY
ACCOO
CLUMON
TAISER
We're leaving!
Sit down!
HOW THE LAW STUDENTS EXPRESSED THEIR DISPLEASURE.

Now arrange the circled letters to form the surprise answer, as suggested by the above cartoon.

Print answer here WITH A " "

PUZZLE
63

JUMBLE®

Unscramble these four Jumbles, one letter to each square, to form four ordinary words.

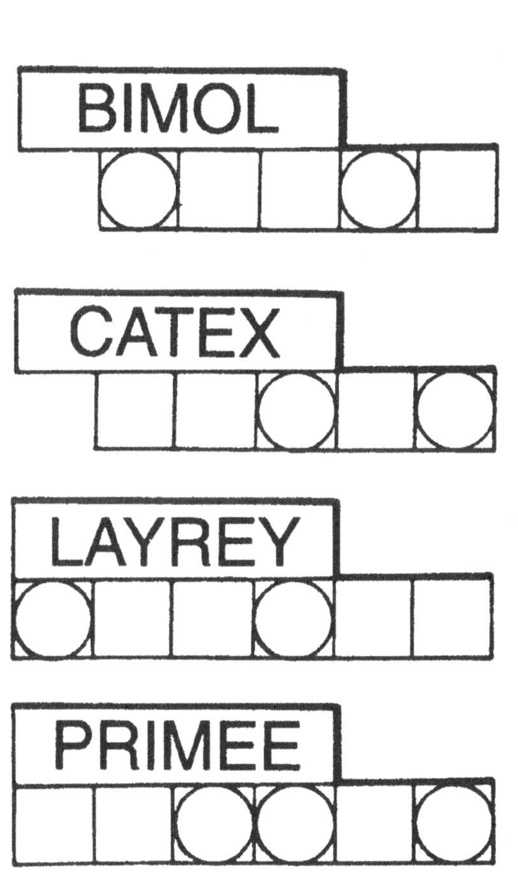
BIMOL
CATEX
LAYREY
PRIMEE

WHAT THE ACTOR'S HANDYMAN ROLE MADE HIM FEEL LIKE.

Now arrange the circled letters to form the surprise answer, as suggested by the above cartoon.

Print answer here A

PUZZLE
64

JUMBLE®

Unscramble these four Jumbles, one letter to each square, to form four ordinary words.

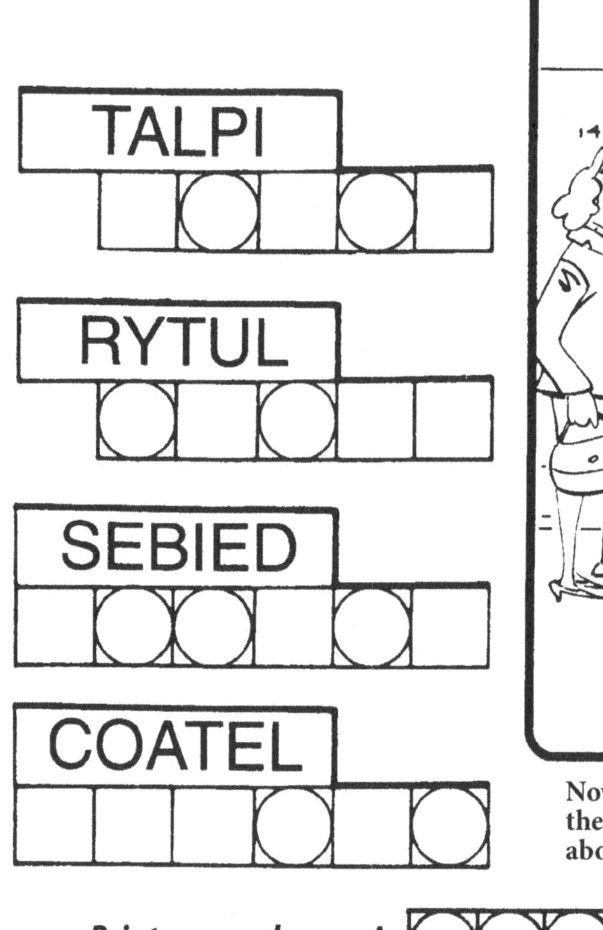
TALPI
RYTUL
SEBIED
COATEL

No additional cost
14 E
WHAT A HOTEL ROOM UPGRADE CAN BECOME.

Now arrange the circled letters to form the surprise answer, as suggested by the above cartoon.

Print answer here A

PUZZLE
65

JUMBLE®

Unscramble these four Jumbles, one letter to each square, to form four ordinary words.

WREEF

TUISE

LEETEY

DIPALL

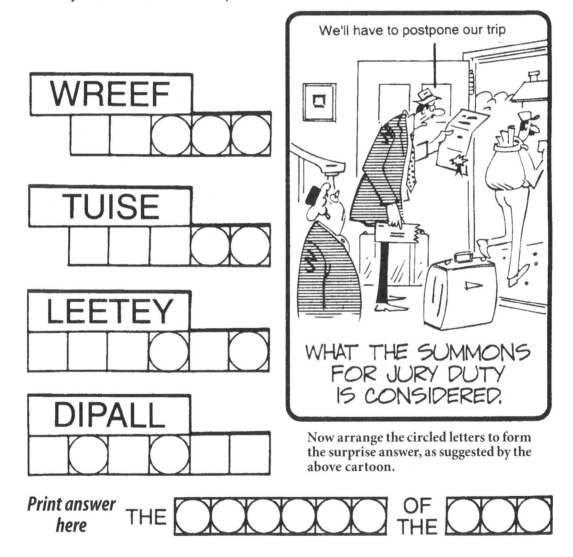

We'll have to postpone our trip

WHAT THE SUMMONS FOR JURY DUTY IS CONSIDERED.

Now arrange the circled letters to form the surprise answer, as suggested by the above cartoon.

Print answer here THE ○○○○○○ OF THE ○○○

PUZZLE
66

JUMBLE®

Unscramble these four Jumbles, one letter to each square, to form four ordinary words.

TOINX
GHILT
KRANET
HELGGA
It's your turn, Jenson
WHAT NEW LUMBER-
JACKS SEEK THAT
THE OTHERS DREAD.

Now arrange the circled letters to form the surprise answer, as suggested by the above cartoon.

Print answer here ○○○○○○○ THE ○○

PUZZLE
67

JUMBLE®

Unscramble these four Jumbles, one letter to each square, to form four ordinary words.

STEAE
KNALF
SMIFLY
SPOGLE
HOW THE SHOEMAKERS DESCRIBED THEMSELVES.

Now arrange the circled letters to form the surprise answer, as suggested by the above cartoon.

Print answer here

PUZZLE
68

JUMBLE®

Unscramble these four Jumbles, one letter to each square, to form four ordinary words.

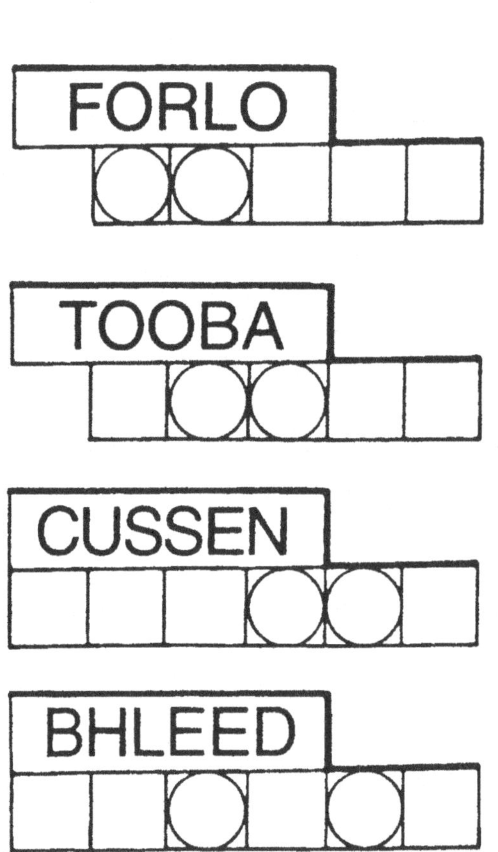
FORLO
TOOBA
CUSSEN
BHLEED

She's so quiet
WHY THE TIRED PARTY-GOER WANTED TO LEAVE.

Now arrange the circled letters to form the surprise answer, as suggested by the above cartoon.

Print answer here SHE WAS

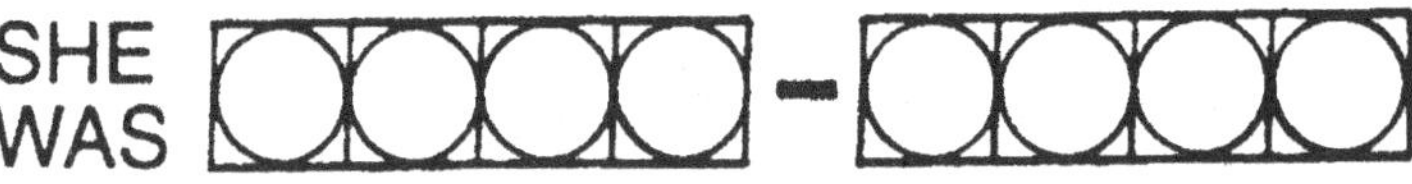

PUZZLE
69

JUMBLE

Unscramble these four Jumbles, one letter to each square, to form four ordinary words.

MERIC
BUJOM
NOOMIK
SCOFIA
WHAT HE LOVED MOST ON THE RADIO.

Now arrange the circled letters to form the surprise answer, as suggested by the above cartoon.

Print answer here “ ”

PUZZLE
70

JUMBLE®

Unscramble these four Jumbles, one letter to each square, to form four ordinary words.

LOJYL
MOPET
TERVID
CAPELA
Fifi never listens
She will
WHAT SHE CONSIDERED HER DOG'S OBEDIENCE TRAINING.
Now arrange the circled letters to form the surprise answer, as suggested by the above cartoon.
Print answer here
HER

PUZZLE
71

JUMBLE®

Unscramble these four Jumbles, one letter to each square, to form four ordinary words.

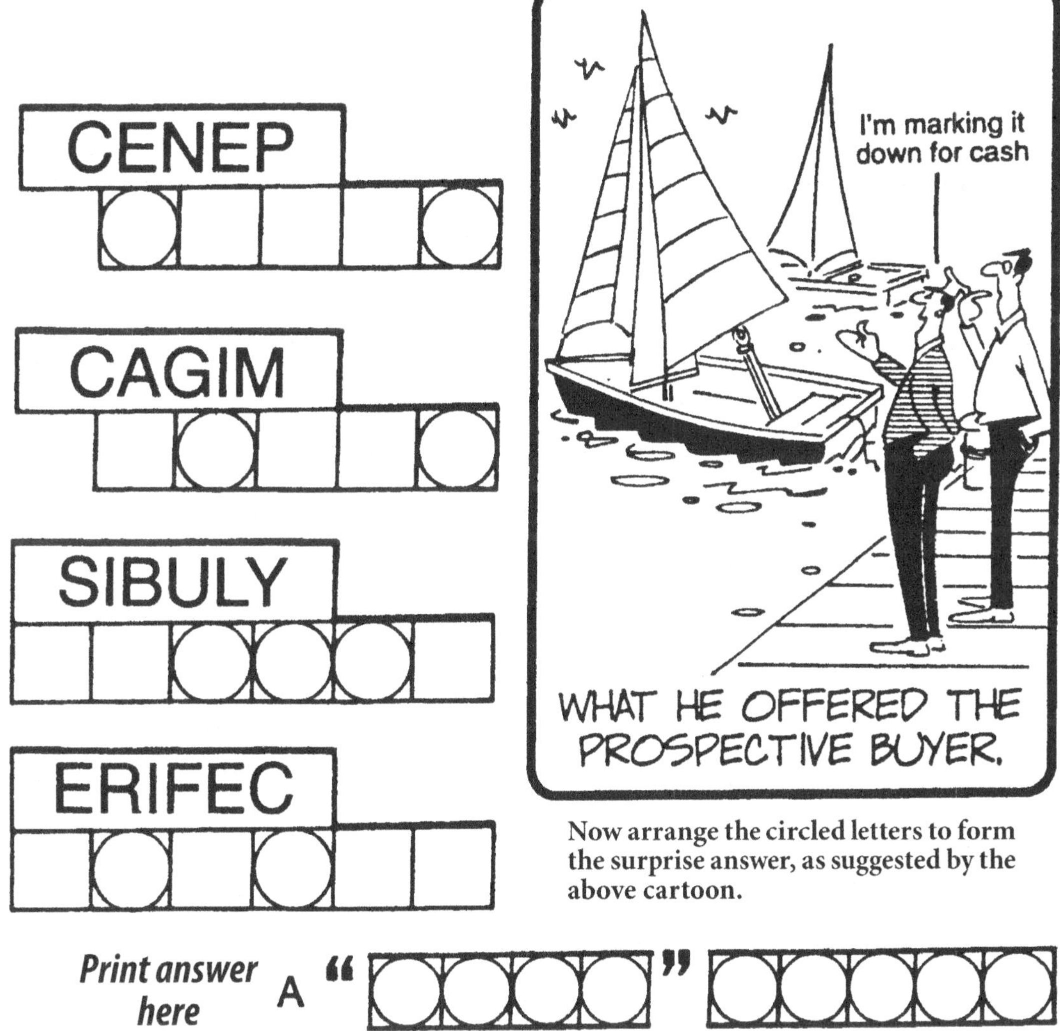
CENEP
CAGIM
SIBULY
ERIFEC
I'm marking it down for cash
WHAT HE OFFERED THE PROSPECTIVE BUYER.

Now arrange the circled letters to form the surprise answer, as suggested by the above cartoon.

Print answer here A " "

PUZZLE
72

JUMBLE®

Unscramble these four Jumbles, one letter to each square, to form four ordinary words.

BIGEE
KIRPE
BRAFIC
TRAFOC
HOW SHE DESCRIBED HER MORNING IN RUSH HOUR.

Now arrange the circled letters to form the surprise answer, as suggested by the above cartoon.

Print answer here

PUZZLE
73

JUMBLE®

Unscramble these four Jumbles, one letter to each square, to form four ordinary words.

IPSOE

UPYPP

TIQUEY

MUSCLY

You want me to polish the top?

WHAT THE BARBER WAS NOTED FOR.

Now arrange the circled letters to form the surprise answer, as suggested by the above cartoon.

Print answer here HIS " ◯◯◯◯ ◯◯◯◯◯ "

PUZZLE
74

JUMBLE®

Unscramble these four Jumbles, one letter to each square, to form four ordinary words.

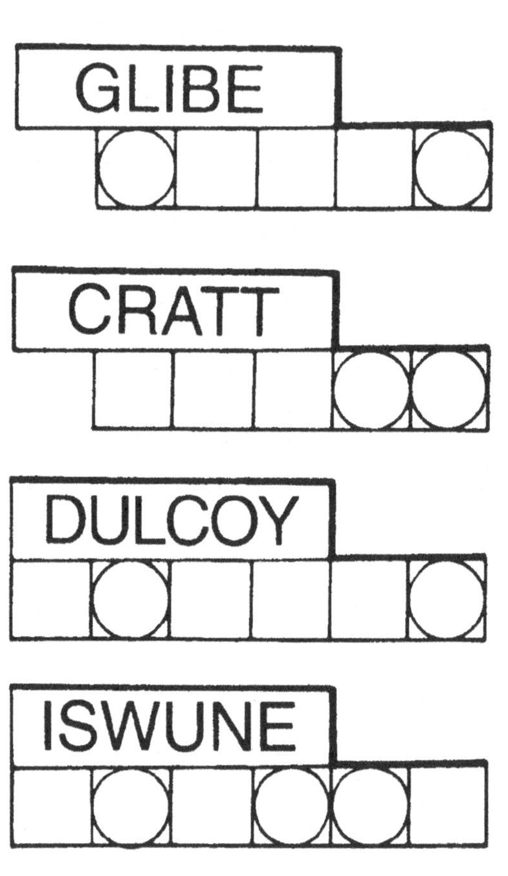

GLIBE
CRATT
DULCOY
ISWUNE

SAVE
50%

HOW THE FRUGAL SHOPPER MADE HER PURCHASING DECISIONS.

Now arrange the circled letters to form the surprise answer, as suggested by the above cartoon.

Print answer here " ◯◯◯◯◯ ' - ◯◯◯◯◯ "

PUZZLE
75

JUMBLE®

Unscramble these four Jumbles, one letter to each square, to form four ordinary words.

LIBEE
LATAN
BENAMO
THEESE
May I see you after the show?
WHEN THE SCOUNDREL DANCED WITH THE BALLERINA, IT WAS--

Now arrange the circled letters to form the surprise answer, as suggested by the above cartoon.

Print answer here ◯◯◯◯ TO ◯◯◯

PUZZLE
76

JUMBLE®

Unscramble these four Jumbles, one letter to each square, to form four ordinary words.

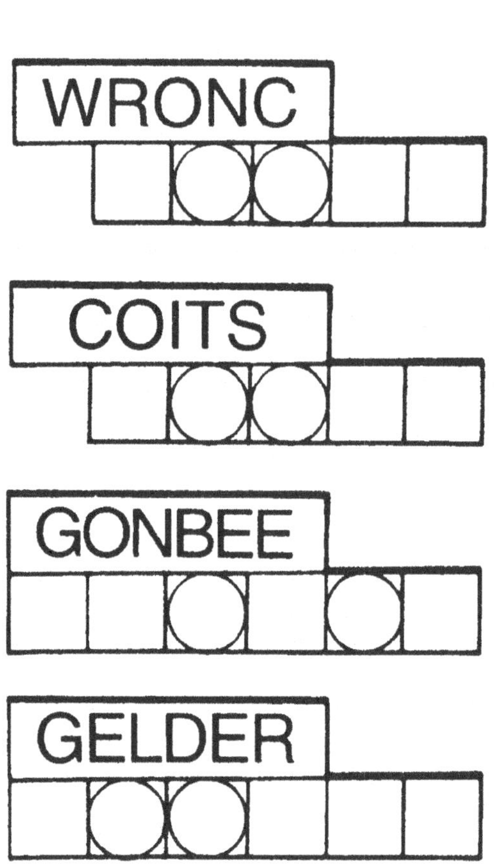
WRONC
COITS
GONBEE
GELDER

Land must be straight ahead
WHAT THE SHIPWRECKED CREW CALLED THE BIRD'S VISIT.

Now arrange the circled letters to form the surprise answer, as suggested by the above cartoon.

Print answer here A "◯◯◯◯◯ ◯◯◯◯◯"

PUZZLE
77

JUMBLE®

Unscramble these four Jumbles, one letter to each square, to form four ordinary words.

VELGA
DUNET
CYSTOL
DACRIN
Listen to me
WHAT THE COACH GAVE THE CHANNEL SWIMMERS.

Now arrange the circled letters to form the surprise answer, as suggested by the above cartoon.

Print answer here " "

PUZZLE
78

JUMBLE®

Unscramble these four Jumbles, one letter to each square, to form four ordinary words.

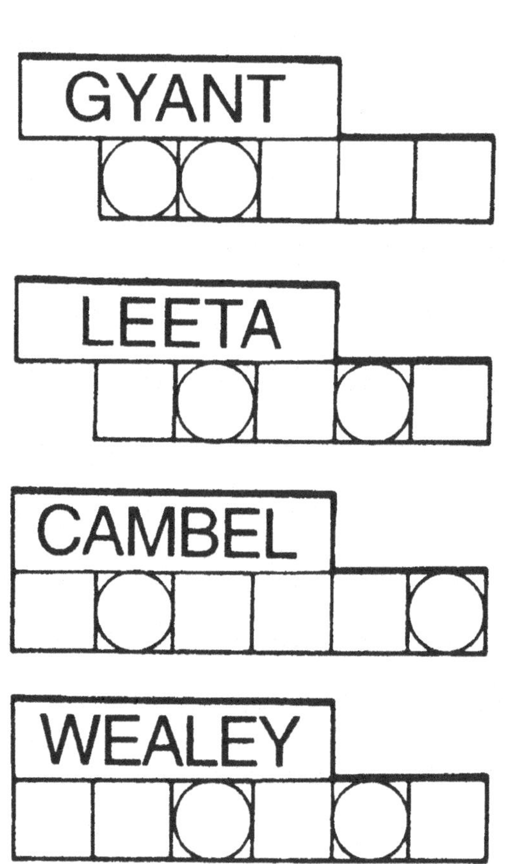
GYANT
LEETA
CAMBEL
WEALEY

It's practically time for breakfast
WHAT THE AUSTRALIAN WIFE CALLED HER TARDY HUSBAND.

Now arrange the circled letters to form the surprise answer, as suggested by the above cartoon.

Print answer here HER  

PUZZLE
79

JUMBLE®

Unscramble these four Jumbles, one letter to each square, to form four ordinary words.

KEHRI
TYSUL
COBIED
CRUVSY
This one is used by all the folks in the big town
WHAT THE RURAL VISITOR FOUND IN THE URBAN STORE.

Now arrange the circled letters to form the surprise answer, as suggested by the above cartoon.

Print answer here A

PUZZLE
80

JUMBLE®

Unscramble these four Jumbles, one letter to each square, to form four ordinary words.

CEDDI
DACKE
COWLAL
UNTRAB
One more notch to go
HOW SHE SUCCEEDED ON HER DIET.
Print answer here
SHE

Now arrange the circled letters to form the surprise answer, as suggested by the above cartoon.

PUZZLE
81

JUMBLE®

Unscramble these four Jumbles, one letter to each square, to form four ordinary words.

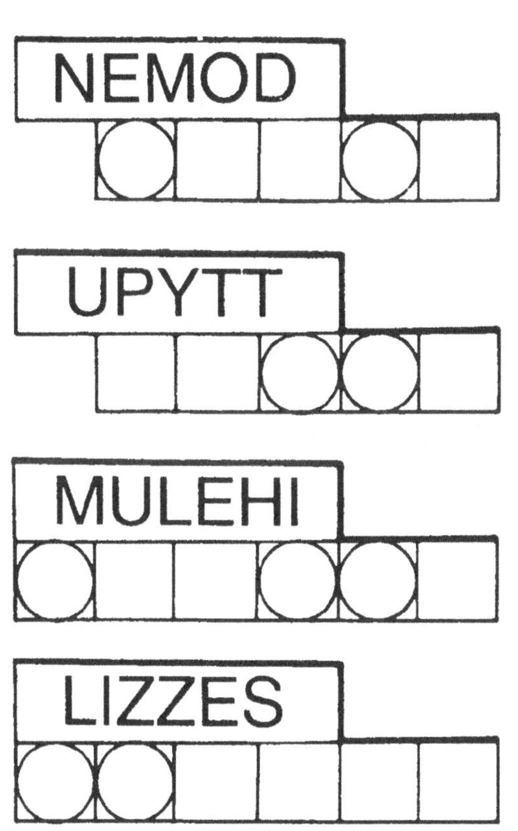
NEMOD
UPYTT
MULEHI
LIZZES

You're right as always, dear
!
HE NEVER FOUGHT WITH HIS WIFE BECAUSE SHE KNEW HOW TO ---

Now arrange the circled letters to form the surprise answer, as suggested by the above cartoon.

Print answer here

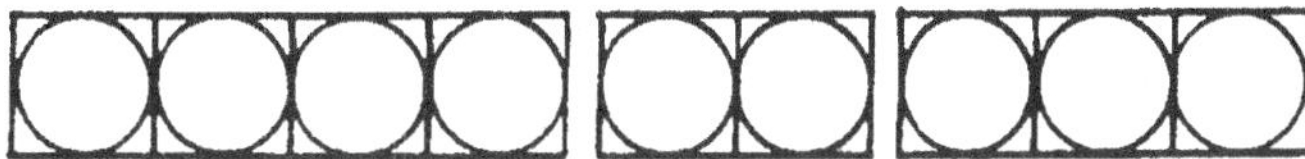

PUZZLE
82

JUMBLE®

Unscramble these four Jumbles, one letter to each square, to form four ordinary words.

OSKET
STUCO
HACTLE
NORREC
WHAT THE
ELECTRICIAN SAID
THE MOVIE WAS.

Now arrange the circled letters to form the surprise answer, as suggested by the above cartoon.

Print answer here A

JUMBLE®

Unscramble these four Jumbles, one letter to each square, to form four ordinary words.

LEWJE

SARBS

CARECS

CITIEL

Finest collection in town
WHAT THE WRITER ON EXOTIC WINES WAS KNOWN FOR HAVING.

Now arrange the circled letters to form the surprise answer, as suggested by the above cartoon.

THE " "

PUZZLE
84

JUMBLE®

Unscramble these four Jumbles, one letter to each square, to form four ordinary words.

INCCY
REVNY
LOACCI
GENNIE
It'll be as good as new
ANOTHER NAME FOR RESTORING A BROKEN BIKE.

Now arrange the circled letters to form the surprise answer, as suggested by the above cartoon.

Print answer here

PUZZLE
85

JUMBLE®

Unscramble these four Jumbles, one letter to each square, to form four ordinary words.

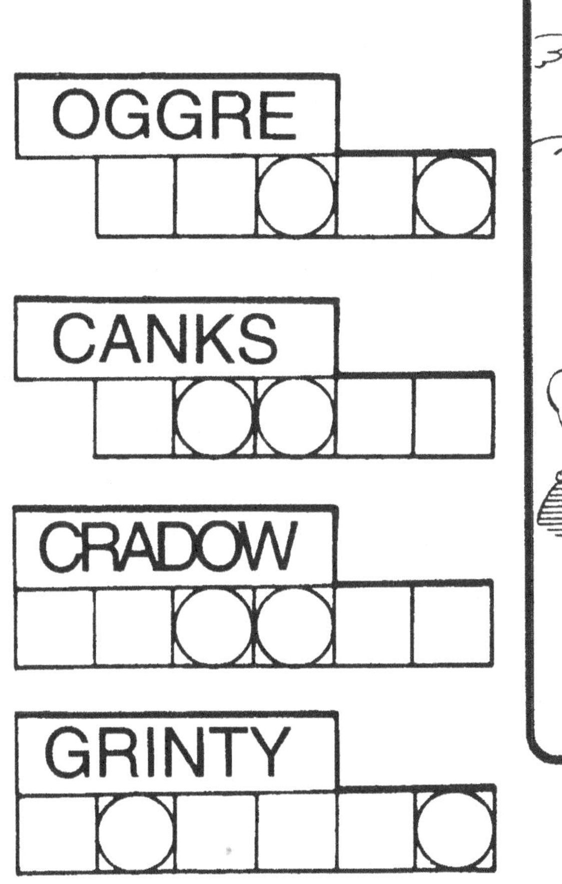
OGGRE
CANKS
CRADOW
GRINTY

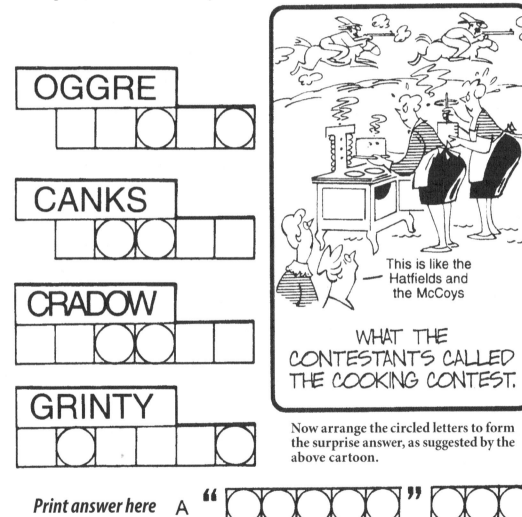

This is like the Hatfields and the McCoys
WHAT THE CONTESTANTS CALLED THE COOKING CONTEST.

Now arrange the circled letters to form the surprise answer, as suggested by the above cartoon.

Print answer here A " ☐☐☐☐☐ " ☐☐☐

PUZZLE
86

JUMBLE®

Unscramble these four Jumbles, one letter to each square, to form four ordinary words.

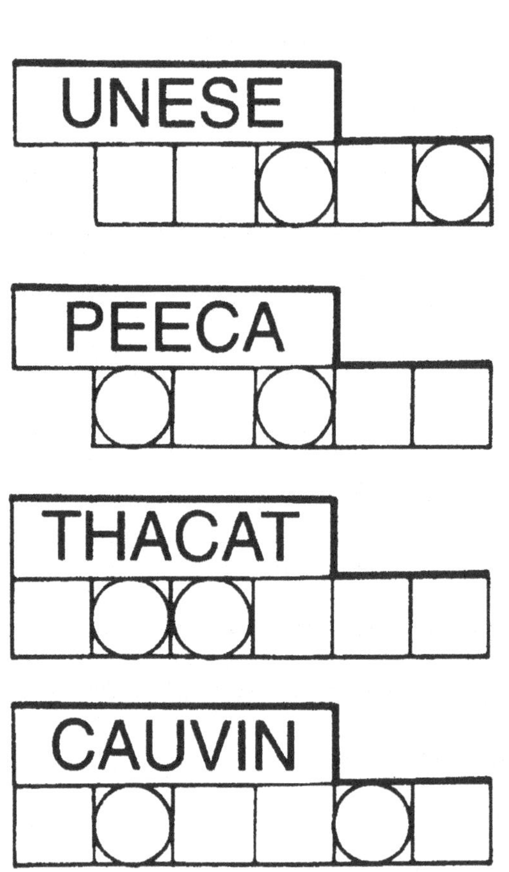

UNESE
PEECA
THACAT
CAUVIN

Next!
WHAT THE CROTCHETY DOCTOR LACKED.

Now arrange the circled letters to form the surprise answer, as suggested by the above cartoon.

Print answer here " "

PUZZLE
87

JUMBLE®

Unscramble these four Jumbles, one letter to each square, to form four ordinary words.

DOLFO
WONGI
HOGNIM
DOUSTI
Keep it up, and you'll make it big someday
ABE LINCOLN'S SUCCESS WAS FUELED BY THIS.

Now arrange the circled letters to form the surprise answer, as suggested by the above cartoon.

Print answer here

PUZZLE
88

JUMBLE®

Unscramble these four Jumbles, one letter to each square, to form four ordinary words.

RISUV

BREYD

ENBAUT

TURAIN

ANOTHER NAME FOR AN ALTAR.

Now arrange the circled letters to form the surprise answer, as suggested by the above cartoon.

Print answer here A

PUZZLE
89

JUMBLE®

Unscramble these four Jumbles, one letter to each square, to form four ordinary words.

NIYKK
WENIT
JELOTS
LOAPER
Here's how Shakespeare would have handled this
17
WHY THE DRAMA TEACHER BECAME A COACH.
Now arrange the circled letters to form the surprise answer, as suggested by the above cartoon.
Print answer here
HE
THE “ ”

PUZZLE
90

JUMBLE®

Unscramble these four Jumbles, one letter to each square, to form four ordinary words.

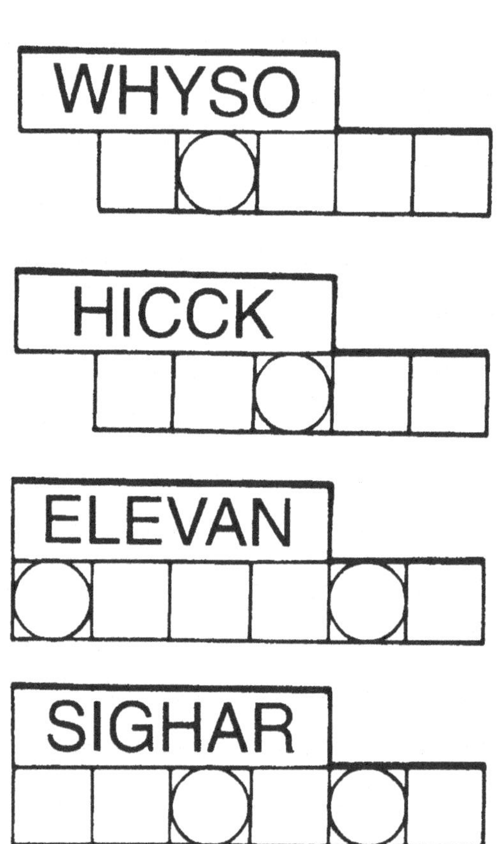
WHYSO
HICCK
ELEVAN
SIGHAR

You're gonna love this!
HOW THE HOT DOG VENDOR HANDLED HIS JOB.

Now arrange the circled letters to form the surprise answer, as suggested by the above cartoon.

Print answer here WITH ""

PUZZLE
91

JUMBLE®

Unscramble these four Jumbles, one letter to each square, to form four ordinary words.

MOBOL
BYGAG
HOMARI
CLEFEE
COMBINE CLASSICAL AND POPULAR MUSIC AND YOU GET THIS.

Now arrange the circled letters to form the surprise answer, as suggested by the above cartoon.

Print answer here ( ) AND ( )

PUZZLE
92

JUMBLE®

Unscramble these four Jumbles, one letter to each square, to form four ordinary words.

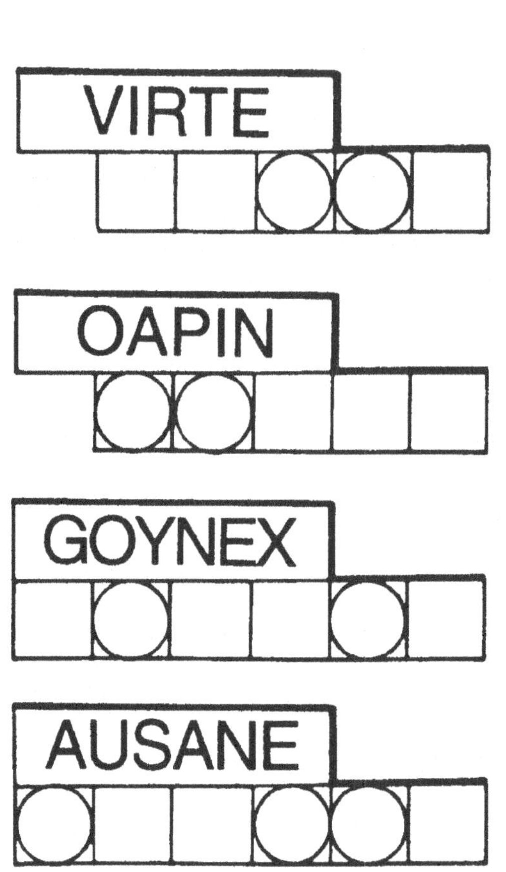
VIRTE
OAPIN
GOYNEX
AUSANE

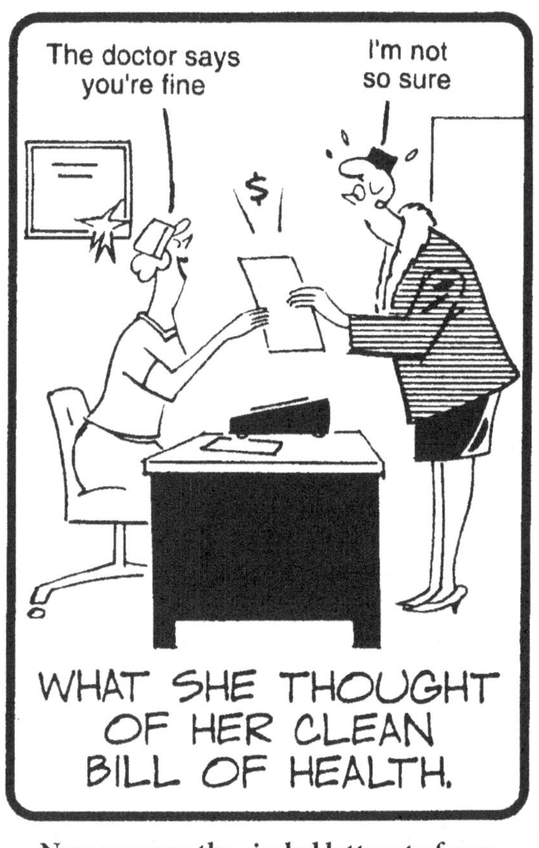
The doctor says you're fine
I'm not so sure
$
WHAT SHE THOUGHT OF HER CLEAN BILL OF HEALTH.

Now arrange the circled letters to form the surprise answer, as suggested by the above cartoon.

Print answer here " "

PUZZLE
93

JUMBLE®
Unscramble these four Jumbles, one letter to each square, to form four ordinary words.
LAWRD
LEVOG
NOBENT
KANTIE
THAT CHARMING MOVIE STAR WAS AS LIKABLE AS SHE WAS THIS.
Now arrange the circled letters to form the surprise answer, as suggested by the above cartoon.

Print answer here “ ”

PUZZLE
94

JUMBLE®

Unscramble these four Jumbles, one letter to each square, to form four ordinary words.

MAUCS
SIPOU
NOMOIK
TEPLYN
WHAT A GOOD GUITARIST MIGHT HAVE.
Now arrange the circled letters to form the surprise answer, as suggested by the above cartoon.
Print answer here
“ ’ ”

PUZZLE
95

JUMBLE®

Unscramble these four Jumbles, one letter to each square, to form four ordinary words.

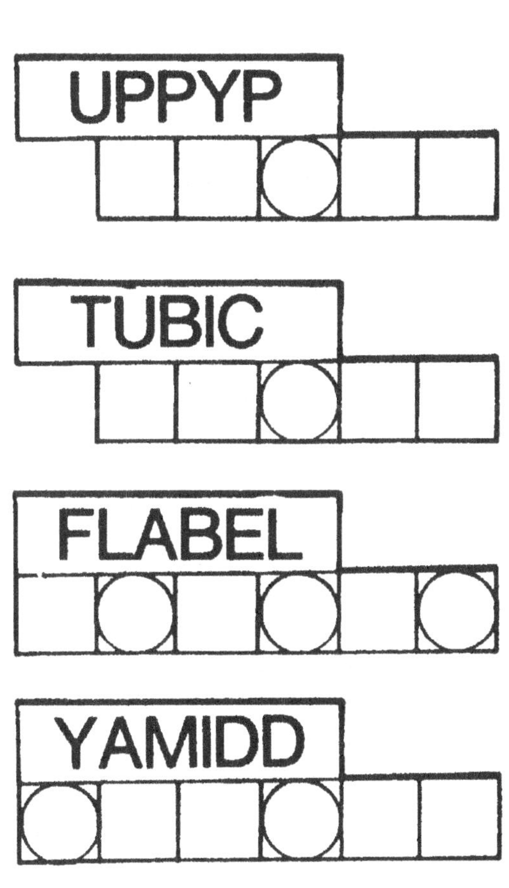

UPPYYP
TUBIC
FLABEL
YAMIDD

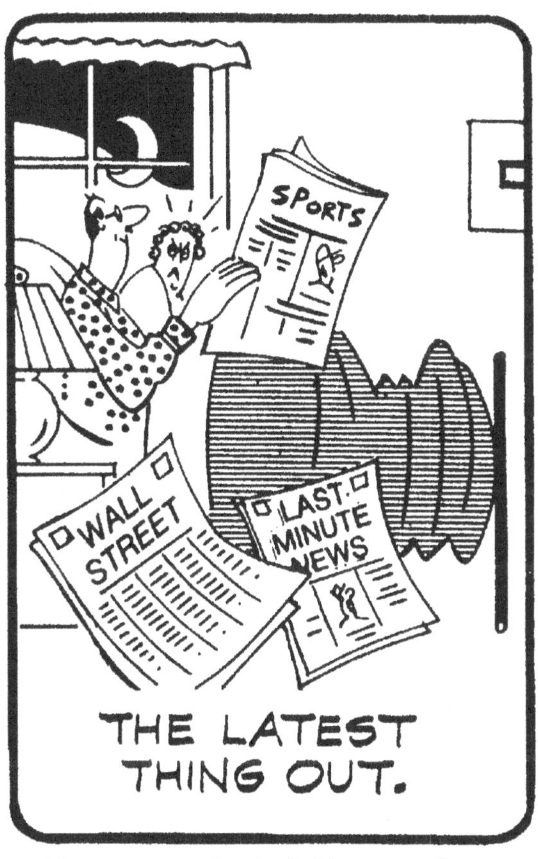

SPORTS
WALL STREET
LAST MINUTE NEWS
THE LATEST THING OUT.

Now arrange the circled letters to form the surprise answer, as suggested by the above cartoon.

Print answer here THE

PUZZLE
96

JUMBLE®

Unscramble these four Jumbles, one letter to each square, to form four ordinary words.

BYGUL

SUPEA

ORMOAN

WHERDS

HOW BALLET HAS GROWN IN POPULARITY IN RECENT YEARS.

Now arrange the circled letters to form the surprise answer, as suggested by the above cartoon.

Print answer here BY &

PUZZLE
97

JUMBLE®

Unscramble these four Jumbles, one letter to each square, to form four ordinary words.

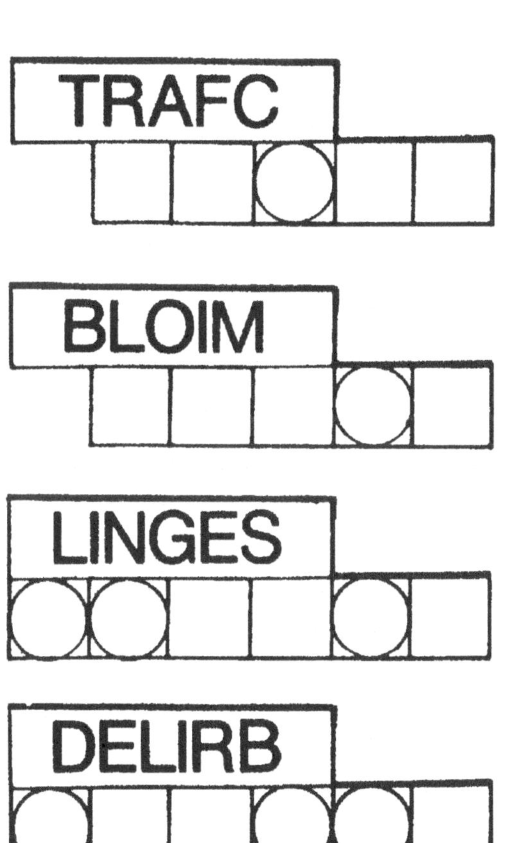
TRAFC
BLOIM
LINGES
DELIRB

A free trip to the moon for everybody!
WHAT A COUNTER-FEITER TURNED POLITICIAN MIGHT BE EXPECTED TO PASS.

Now arrange the circled letters to form the surprise answer, as suggested by the above cartoon.

Print answer here

PUZZLE
98

JUMBLE®

Unscramble these four Jumbles, one letter to each square, to form four ordinary words.

HAFFC

YAILG

NOALOS

PHELER

ANOTHER FORM OF VERBAL ABUSE.

Now arrange the circled letters to form the surprise answer, as suggested by the above cartoon.

Print answer here " "

JUMBLE®

Unscramble these four Jumbles, one letter to each square, to form four ordinary words.

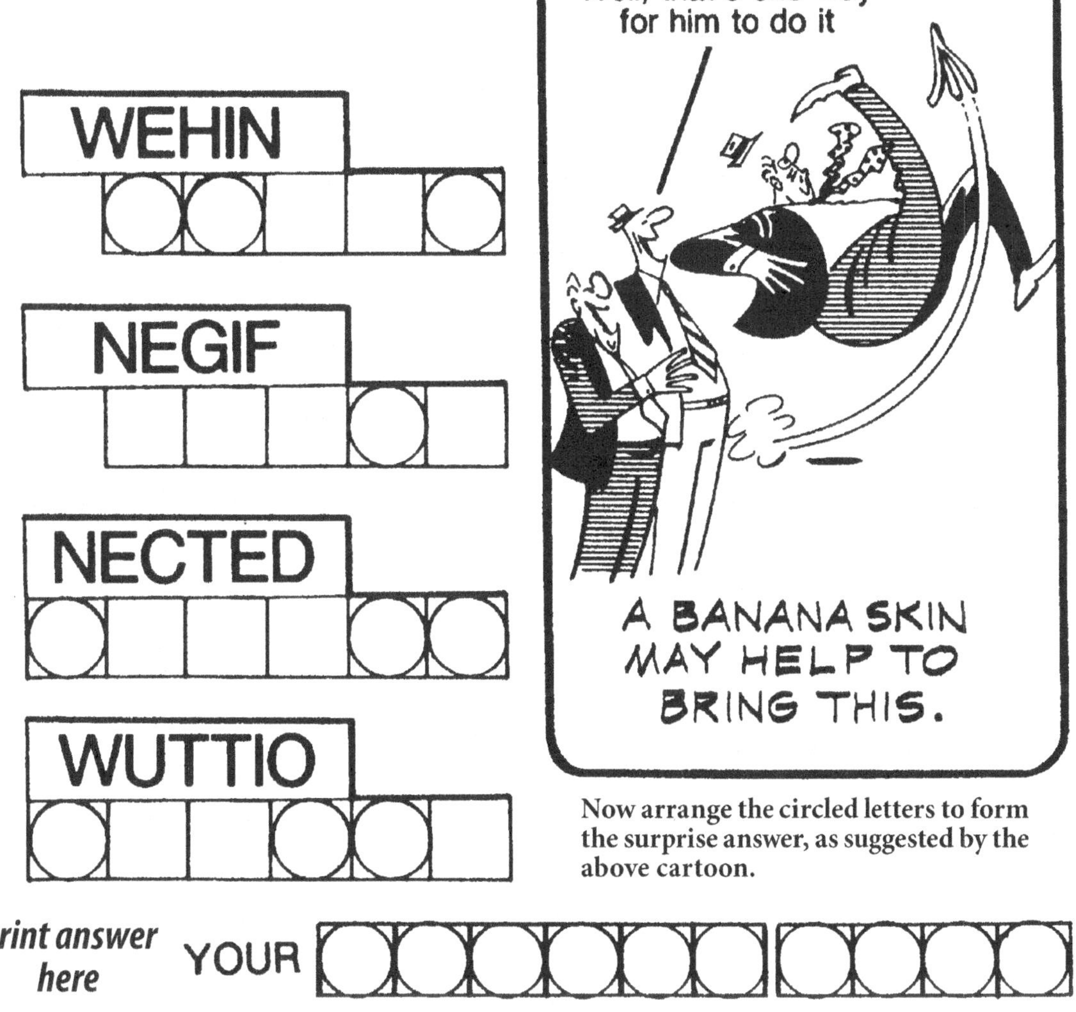
WEHIN
NEGIF
NECTED
WUTTIO
Well, that's one way for him to do it
A BANANA SKIN MAY HELP TO BRING THIS.

Now arrange the circled letters to form the surprise answer, as suggested by the above cartoon.

Print answer here YOUR

PUZZLE
100

JUMBLE®

Unscramble these four Jumbles, one letter to each square, to form four ordinary words.

UMTAG
RAIFE
SHOCUL
SAYILE
WHAT THEIR EFFORTS AT STEALING APPLES WERE.

Now arrange the circled letters to form the surprise answer, as suggested by the above cartoon.

Print answer here

PUZZLE
101

JUMBLE®

Unscramble these four Jumbles, one letter to each square, to form four ordinary words.

YOCEV

CUMIS

KRAYBE

RODION

How charming and carefree

WHAT THEY SAID ABOUT THE SOCIETY GIRL THE FIRST TIME SHE APPEARED ON TV.

Now arrange the circled letters to form the surprise answer, as suggested by the above cartoon.

Print answer here " ◯◯◯ - ◯◯ - ◯◯◯ "

PUZZLE
102

JUMBLE®

Unscramble these four Jumbles, one letter to each square, to form four ordinary words.

JOANB
THEFY
CALKAJ
SLIZZE
WANTED
WHAT A COWARD MIGHT DO WHEN HE GETS INTO A "JAM."
Now arrange the circled letters to form the surprise answer, as suggested by the above cartoon.
Print answer here
LIKE

PUZZLE
103

JUMBLE®

Unscramble these four Jumbles, one letter to each square, to form four ordinary words.

ALVAN

NIFTE

UNBART

TALCOE

Please!
Please!
WHAT THE CON-FIRMED BACHELOR'S VIEWS WERE.

Now arrange the circled letters to form the surprise answer, as suggested by the above cartoon.

Print answer here "◯◯-◯◯◯◯◯◯-◯◯◯◯◯"

PUZZLE
104

JUMBLE®

Unscramble these four Jumbles, one letter to each square, to form four ordinary words.

TEFIB

WOGIN

YORPTS

DARCCO

He never likes the pieces we're doing

REGARDLESS OF WHAT THE ORCHESTRA PERFORMS, THE BASS PLAYER HAS TO DO THIS.

Now arrange the circled letters to form the surprise answer, as suggested by the above cartoon.

Print answer here IT

PUZZLE
105

JUMBLE®

Unscramble these four Jumbles, one letter to each square, to form four ordinary words.

IKKAH
BAEBY
DUNJOC
HELSIG
Have you heard the rumor about him?
AN ACROBAT IS THE ONLY PERSON WHO CAN TALK ABOUT HIMSELF THIS WAY.

Now arrange the circled letters to form the surprise answer, as suggested by the above cartoon.

Print answer here ◯◯◯◯◯◯ HIS OWN ◯◯◯◯

PUZZLE
106

JUMBLE®

Unscramble these four Jumbles, one letter to each square, to form four ordinary words.

INARG

DYADD

YOBUDE

HIMSUL

WHY THE CROOK DISGUISED HIMSELF AS A SHEPHERD.

Now arrange the circled letters to form the surprise answer, as suggested by the above cartoon.

Print answer here ◯◯ WAS ◯◯ THE "◯◯◯◯◯"

PUZZLE
107

JUMBLE®

Unscramble these four Jumbles, one letter to each square, to form four ordinary words.

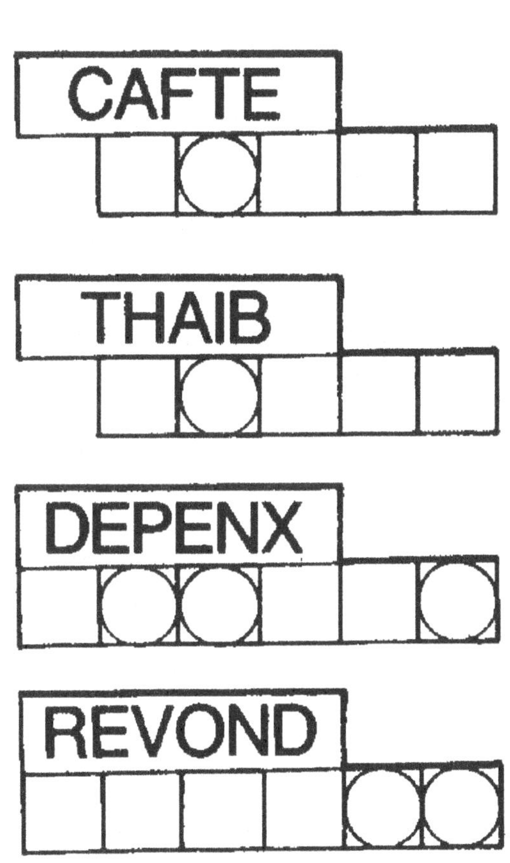
CAFTE
THAIB
DEPENX
REVOND

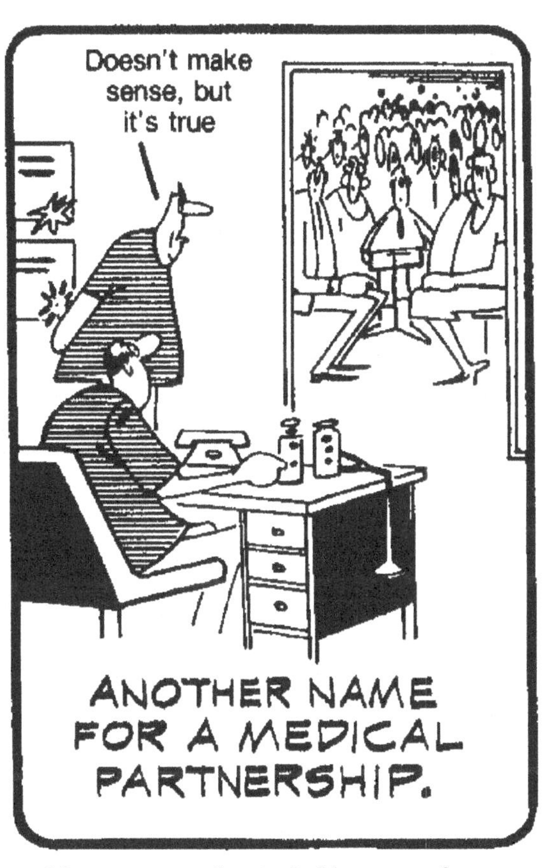
Doesn't make sense, but it's true
ANOTHER NAME FOR A MEDICAL PARTNERSHIP.

Now arrange the circled letters to form the surprise answer, as suggested by the above cartoon.

Print answer here A 

PUZZLE
108

JUMBLE

Unscramble these four Jumbles, one letter to each square, to form four ordinary words.

HARCO

TISUE

DEDAHN

GIFNIX

I hope they've got a job for me

A—E

WHAT THE UNEM-PLOYED BURLESQUE DANCER HAD.

Now arrange the circled letters to form the surprise answer, as suggested by the above cartoon.

Print answer here NO " " TO

PUZZLE
109

JUMBLE®

Unscramble these four Jumbles, one letter to each square, to form four ordinary words.

SARBS

NIRPT

FLUNGE

METIKS

You've got to learn to loosen up

WHAT THE SHRINK'S NERVOUS PATIENT WAS.

Now arrange the circled letters to form the surprise answer, as suggested by the above cartoon.

Print answer here " - "

PUZZLE
110

JUMBLE®

Unscramble these four Jumbles, one letter to each square, to form four ordinary words.

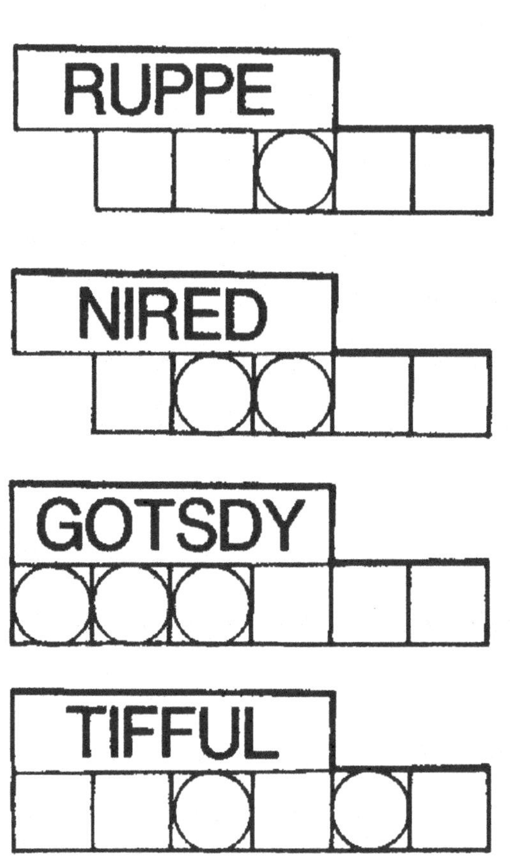
RUPPE
NIRED
GOTSDY
TIFFUL

SHE KNOWS HOW TO GET MORE OUT OF A DRESS THAN THIS.

Now arrange the circled letters to form the surprise answer, as suggested by the above cartoon.

Print answer here SHE ◯◯◯◯ ◯◯◯◯ IT

PUZZLE
111

JUMBLE®

Unscramble these four Jumbles, one letter to each square, to form four ordinary words.

FUTLE
TYKIT
VELPOR
MOUFAS
THE COPS WERE AT THE CROOKS' BARBECUE FOR THIS.

Now arrange the circled letters to form the surprise answer, as suggested by the above cartoon.

Print answer here A " "

PUZZLE
112

JUMBLE®

Unscramble these four Jumbles, one letter to each square, to form four ordinary words.

NONAY
WEDIP
WALLOT
KOJECY
Hope she doesn't call on me
Or me
Or me
THE MOST COMMON ANSWER IN THE CLASS.

Now arrange the circled letters to form the surprise answer, as suggested by the above cartoon.

Print answer here “ ”

PUZZLE
113

JUMBLE®

Unscramble these four Jumbles, one letter to each square, to form four ordinary words.

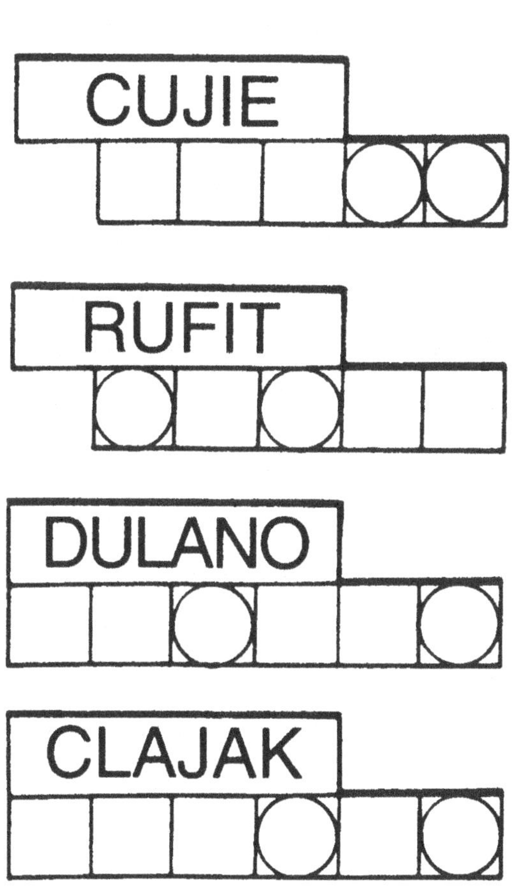
CUJIE
RUFIT
DULANO
CLAJAK

That's not it
Tee Hee—I'm missing a card
Nuts!
THAT CRAZY MAGICIAN SEEMED TO LACK THIS.

Now arrange the circled letters to form the surprise answer, as suggested by the above cartoon.

Print answer here A

PUZZLE
114

JUMBLE®

Unscramble these four Jumbles, one letter to each square, to form four ordinary words.

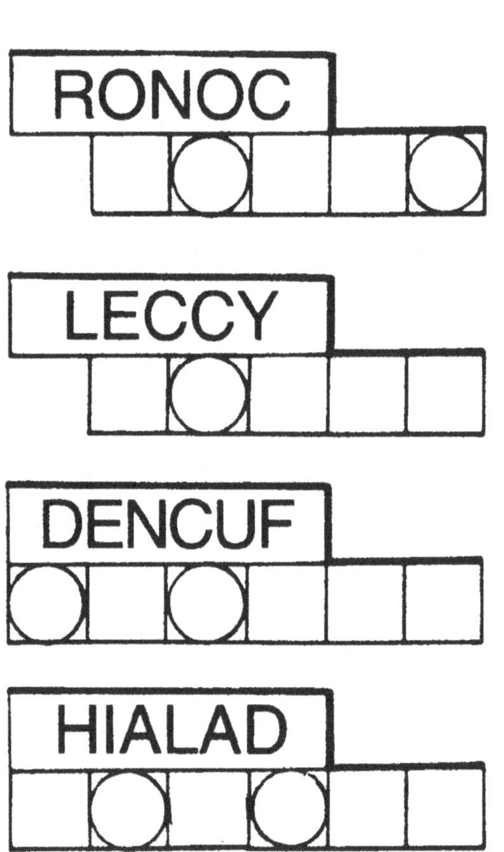
RONOC
LECCY
DENCUF
HIALAD

To be honest, monsieur, we don't trust you
HOW THE FRENCH SOMETIMES CONDUCT LOAN NEGOTIATIONS.

Now arrange the circled letters to form the surprise answer, as suggested by the above cartoon.

Print answer here "◯◯◯◯◯-◯◯"

PUZZLE
115

JUMBLE®

Unscramble these four Jumbles, one letter to each square, to form four ordinary words.

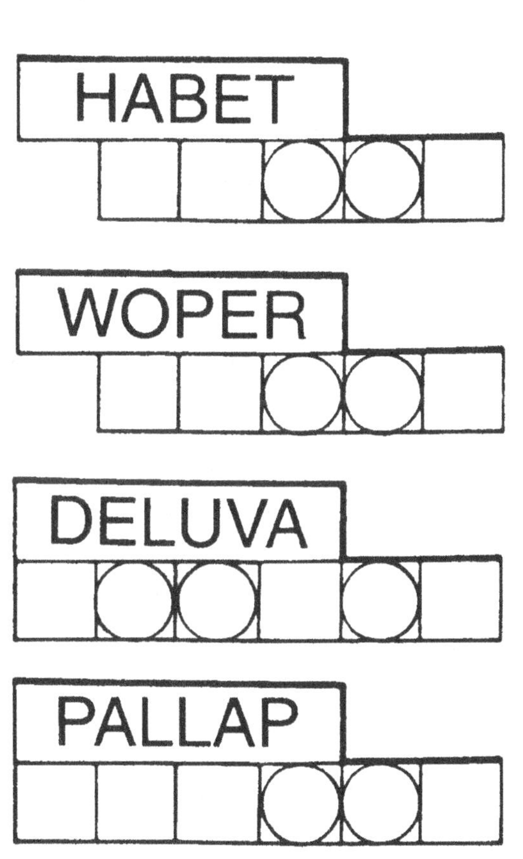
HABET
WOPER
DELUVA
PALLAP

Thar she blows!
WHAT WAS THE STORY ABOUT MOBY DICK?

Now arrange the circled letters to form the surprise answer, as suggested by the above cartoon.

Print answer here A

PUZZLE
116

JUMBLE®

Unscramble these four Jumbles, one letter to each square, to form four ordinary words.

HACCO

DEEKY

RUFUTE

ZEFIRE

It's not running
Neither is the nag
HOW THE TRAINER REACTED TO THE BROKEN STOPWATCH.

Now arrange the circled letters to form the surprise answer, as suggested by the above cartoon.

Print answer here HE WAS "◯◯◯◯◯◯ ◯◯◯◯"

PUZZLE
117

JUMBLE®

Unscramble these four Jumbles, one letter to each square, to form four ordinary words.

YIHFS
DIPEW
CONDES
KELCHE
A TACTFUL HUSBAND ALWAYS REMEMBERS HIS WIFE'S BIRTHDAY BUT FORGETS THIS.

Now arrange the circled letters to form the surprise answer, as suggested by the above cartoon.

Print answer here ☐☐☐☐☐ ☐☐☐ IT ☐☐

PUZZLE
118

JUMBLE®

Unscramble these four Jumbles, one letter to each square, to form four ordinary words.

KANEL
OYLED
LAYDED
HEERIT
WHAT A CRIMINAL WHO FALLS INTO CEMENT HAS TO BE.

Now arrange the circled letters to form the surprise answer, as suggested by the above cartoon.

Print answer here A ○○○○○○○○ ONE

PUZZLE
119

JUMBLE®
Unscramble these four Jumbles, one letter to each square, to form four ordinary words.
TAUID
LEWNY
GRAVEA
RICKYT

The goodies will arrive any minute
WHOM TO CALL IF YOU'RE PLANNING TO GIVE A BANQUET FOR YOUR CAT.

Now arrange the circled letters to form the surprise answer, as suggested by the above cartoon.

Print answer here THE "☐☐☐-☐☐☐☐☐"

PUZZLE
120

JUMBLE®

Unscramble these four Jumbles, one letter to each square, to form four ordinary words.

YONIS
STRON
SHUBIL
VENAHE
I say—very quiet tonight—eh what?
Shhh!
WHAT LIONESSES MIGHT BE.

Now arrange the circled letters to form the surprise answer, as suggested by the above cartoon.

Print answer here " "

PUZZLE
121

JUMBLE®

Unscramble these four Jumbles, one letter to each square, to form four ordinary words.

GALOW
DRYIT
SMILFY
GAROUC
WHAT THE PERCUSSION PLAYER ENJOYED WITH HIS DINNER.
Now arrange the circled letters to form the surprise answer, as suggested by the above cartoon.
Print answer here
“ ”

PUZZLE
122

JUMBLE®

Unscramble these four Jumbles, one letter to each square, to form four ordinary words.

AMLET
BEREL
HAMMEY
RAWSEN
WHAT THE OIL TYCOON SAID WHEN ASKED TO TALK ABOUT THE SOURCE OF HIS WEALTH.

Now arrange the circled letters to form the surprise answer, as suggested by the above cartoon.

Print answer here IT'S ◯◯◯◯◯◯◯ ◯◯ !

PUZZLE
123

JUMBLE®

Unscramble these four Jumbles, one letter to each square, to form four ordinary words.

STALN

LIVIG

RAHWTT

TUSDIP

WHAT THEY SAID ABOUT THE GHOST.

Now arrange the circled letters to form the surprise answer, as suggested by the above cartoon.

Print answer here ◯◯◯◯'◯ THE ◯◯◯◯◯◯◯!

PUZZLE
124

JUMBLE®

Unscramble these four Jumbles, one letter to each square, to form four ordinary words.

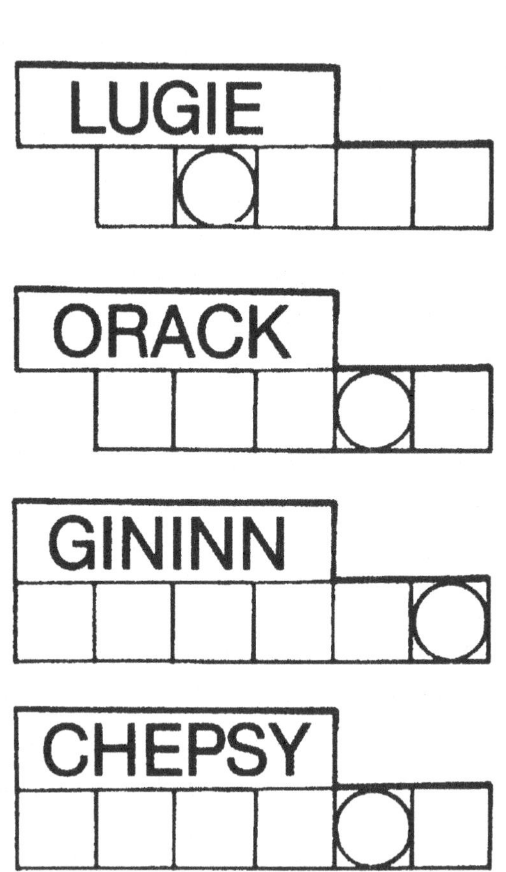
LUGIE
ORACK
GININN
CHEPSY

COULD BE A ROUNDABOUT WAY OF SHOWING YOUR LOVE.

Now arrange the circled letters to form the surprise answer, as suggested by the above cartoon.

Print answer here 

PUZZLE
125

JUMBLE®

Unscramble these four Jumbles, one letter to each square, to form four ordinary words.

NALAB

REMEB

UMCAUV

HARTTO

Boy—is HE wasting his time!
WHAT THEY CALLED THAT GUY WHO WOULDN'T LEND ANY MONEY.

Now arrange the circled letters to form the surprise answer, as suggested by the above cartoon.

Print answer here

PUZZLE
126

JUMBLE®

Unscramble these four Jumbles, one letter to each square, to form four ordinary words.

LYMIF

DALIP

DORFIL

OPPELE

Hey—how do you expect a guy to get any sleep?

WHAT THE ANGRY MUMMY DID.

Now arrange the circled letters to form the surprise answer, as suggested by the above cartoon.

Print answer here HIS

PUZZLE
127

JUMBLE®

Unscramble these four Jumbles, one letter to each square, to form four ordinary words.

TAGUM

LULBY

COPTEK

FLOUJY

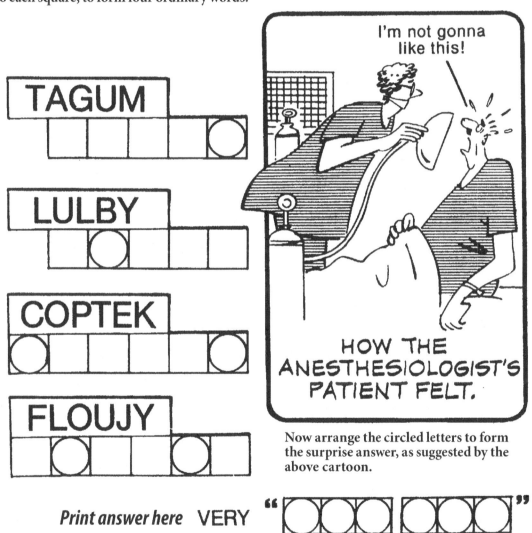

I'm not gonna like this!

HOW THE ANESTHESIOLOGIST'S PATIENT FELT.

Now arrange the circled letters to form the surprise answer, as suggested by the above cartoon.

Print answer here VERY " "

PUZZLE
128

JUMBLE®

Unscramble these four Jumbles, one letter to each square, to form four ordinary words.

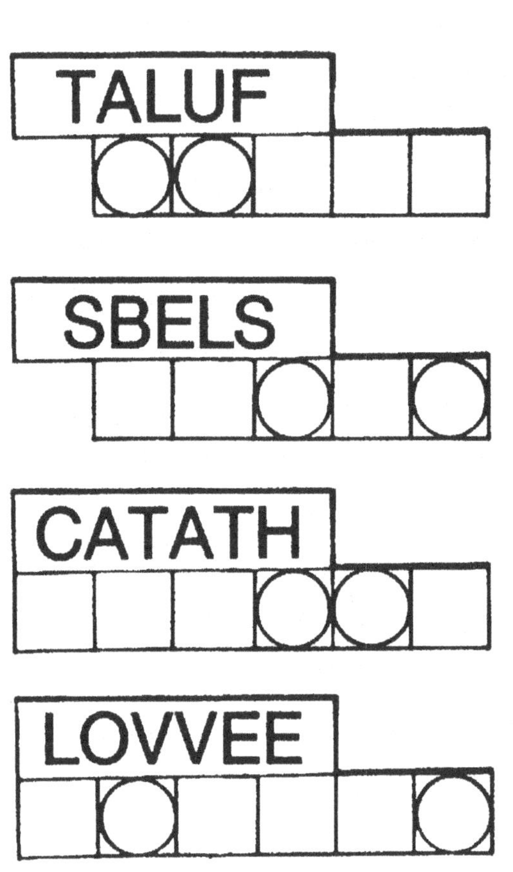
TALUF
SBELS
CATATH
LOVVEE

WHY YOU MIGHT CONSULT A PLASTIC SURGEON.

Now arrange the circled letters to form the surprise answer, as suggested by the above cartoon.

Print answer here TO

PUZZLE
129

JUMBLE®

Unscramble these four Jumbles, one letter to each square, to form four ordinary words.

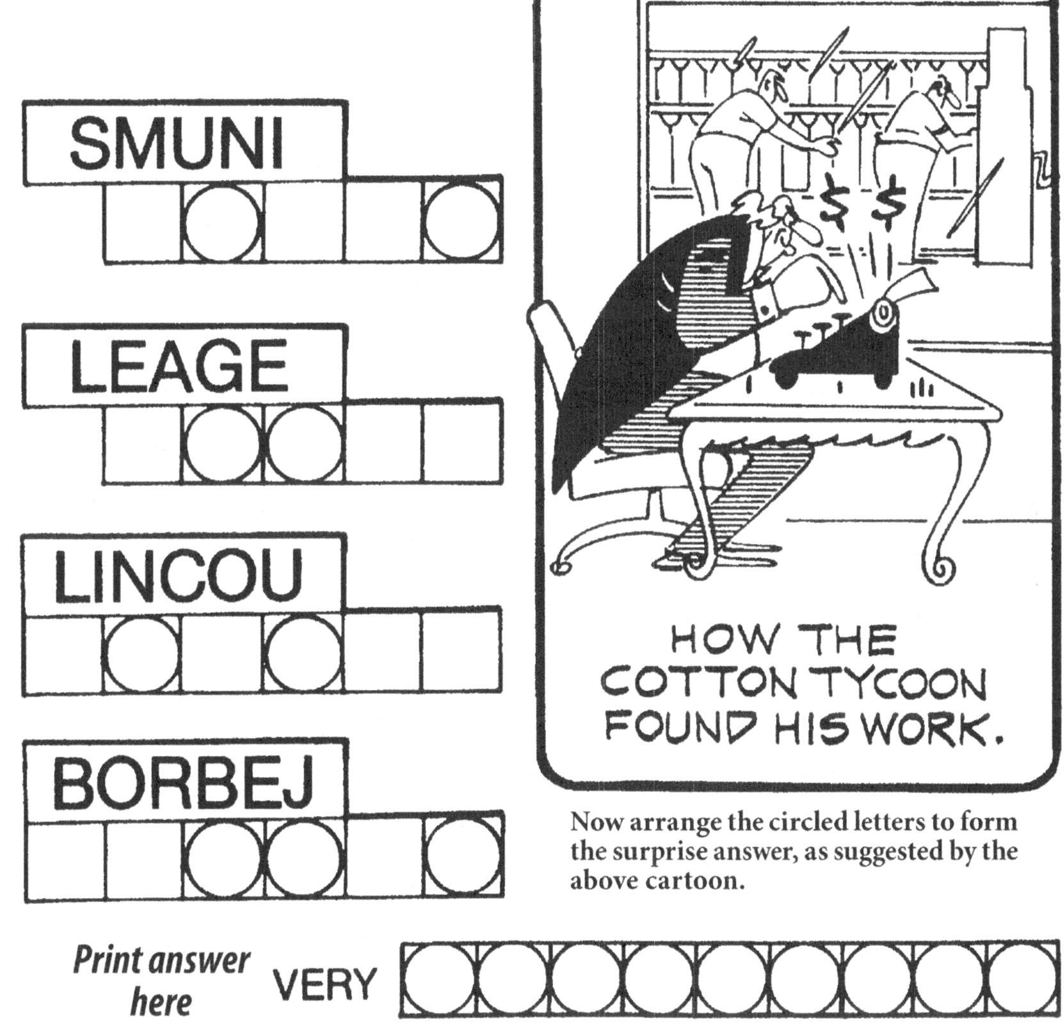
SMUNI
LEAGE
LINCOU
BORBEJ
HOW THE COTTON TYCOON FOUND HIS WORK.
Now arrange the circled letters to form the surprise answer, as suggested by the above cartoon.
Print answer here
VERY

PUZZLE
130

JUMBLE®

Unscramble these four Jumbles, one letter to each square, to form four ordinary words.

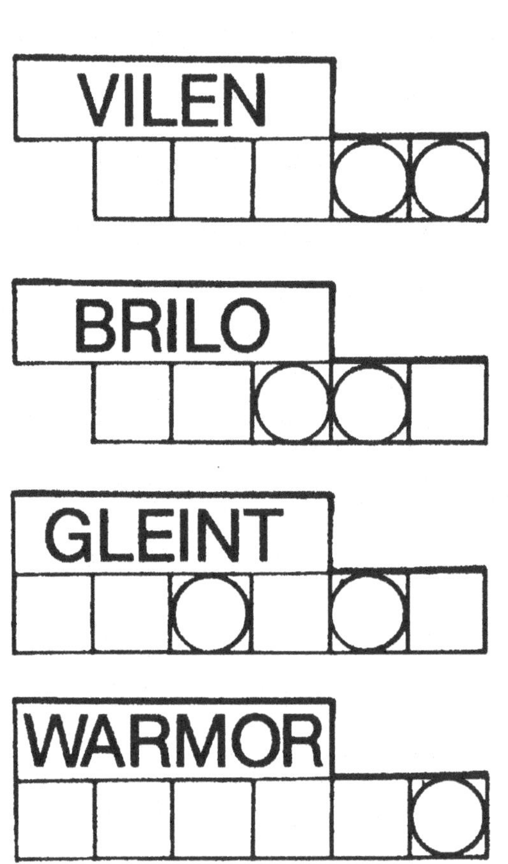
VILEN
BRILO
GLEINT
WARMOR

Really! And is that lipstick on your collar?
HOW THE POOR FISH GOT HOOKED.

Now arrange the circled letters to form the surprise answer, as suggested by the above cartoon.

Print answer here WITH HIS 

PUZZLE
131

JUMBLE®

Unscramble these four Jumbles, one letter to each square, to form four ordinary words.

KNUSK
TULIB
GENPOS
NAUMUT
THEY SAID
THE BACHELOR
WAS NEVER THIS.

Now arrange the circled letters to form the surprise answer, as suggested by the above cartoon.

Print answer here “◯◯◯◯ - ◯◯◯◯◯”

PUZZLE
132

JUMBLE®

Unscramble these four Jumbles, one letter to each square, to form four ordinary words.

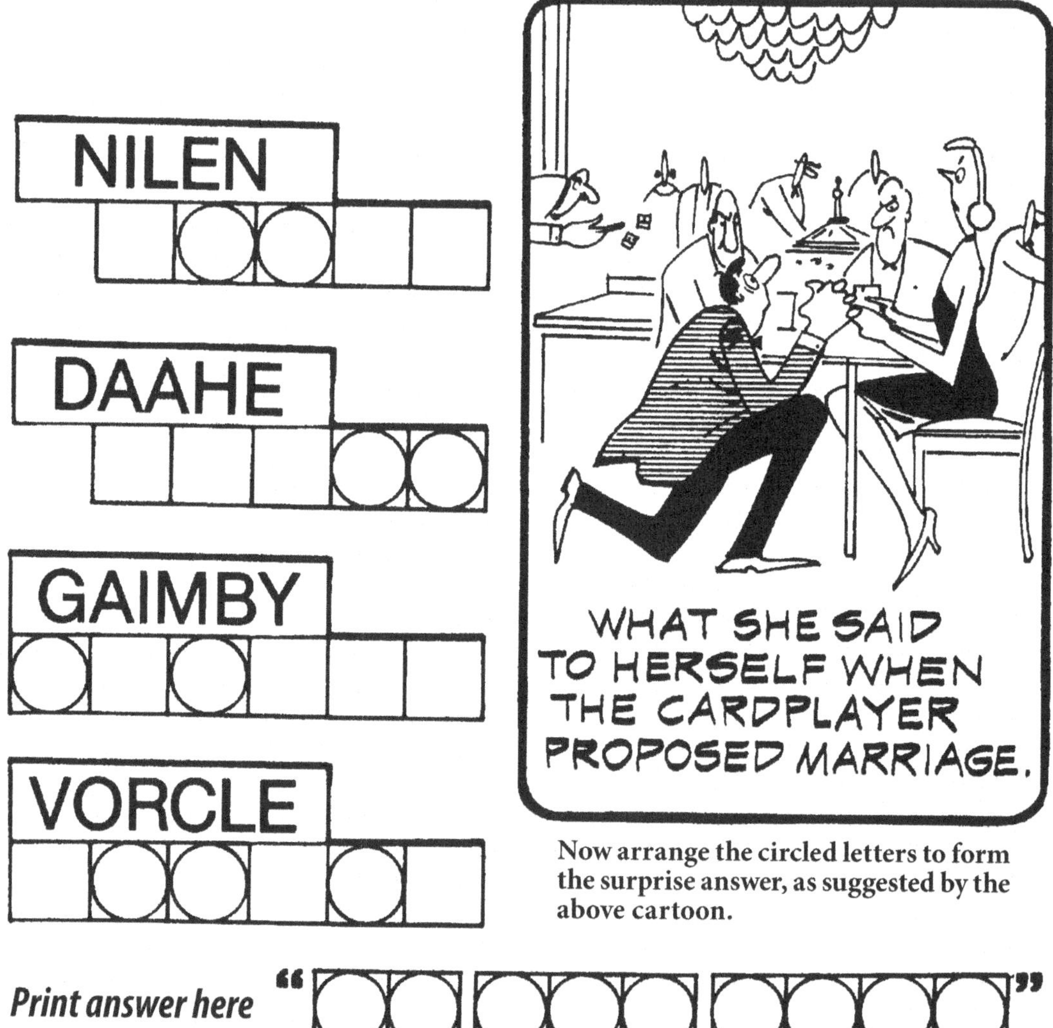
NILEN
DAAHE
GAIMBY
VORCLE
WHAT SHE SAID TO HERSELF WHEN THE CARDPLAYER PROPOSED MARRIAGE.

Now arrange the circled letters to form the surprise answer, as suggested by the above cartoon.

Print answer here " ◯◯ ◯◯◯ ◯◯◯◯◯ "

PUZZLE
133

JUMBLE
LUFAW
WUSAQ
DAYMAL
DELIJA
WHAT THERE SEEMED TO BE IN THAT NOISY COURTROOM.

Unscramble these four Jumbles, one letter to each square, to form four ordinary words.

Now arrange the circled letters to form the surprise answer, as suggested by the above cartoon.

Print answer here MORE " " THAN

PUZZLE
134

JUMBLE®

Unscramble these four Jumbles, one letter to each square, to form four ordinary words.

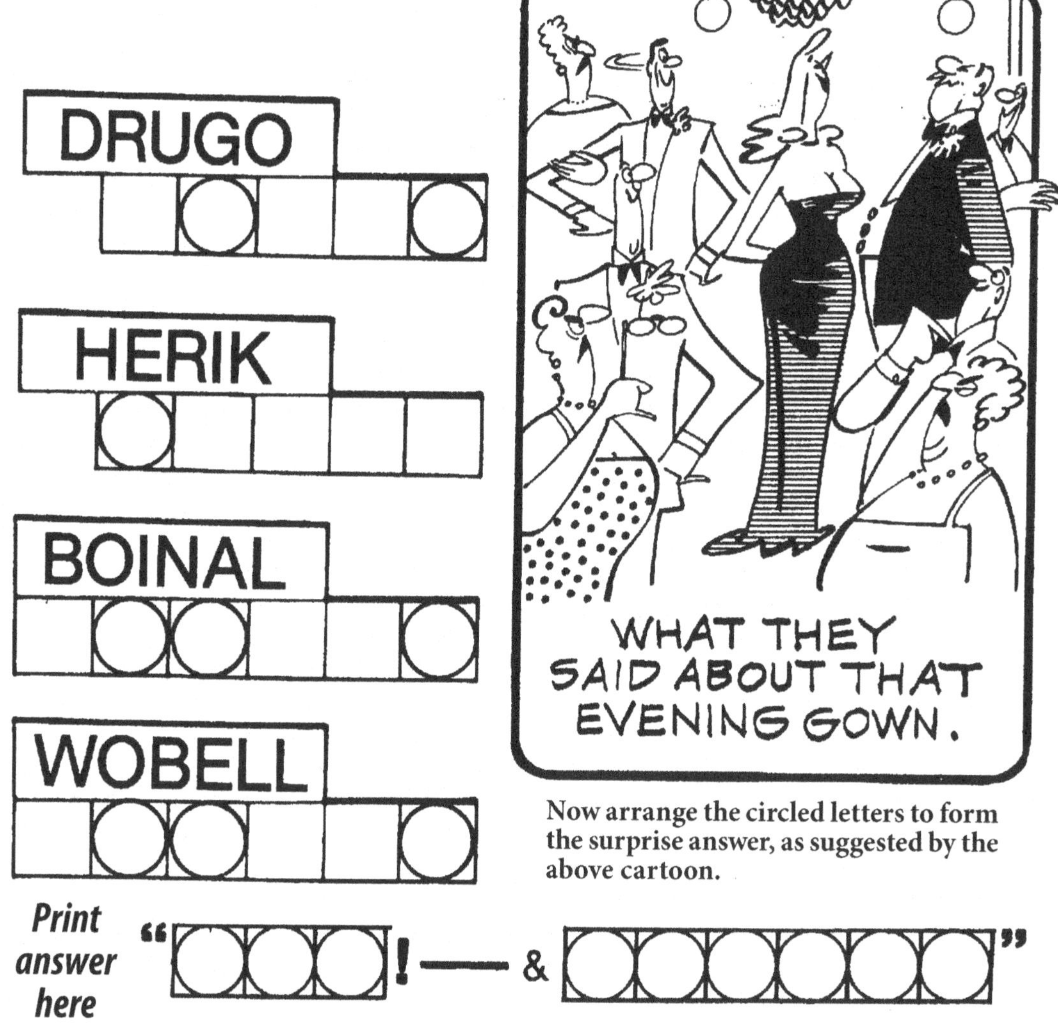
DRUGO
HERIK
BOINAL
WOBELL
WHAT THEY SAID ABOUT THAT EVENING GOWN.

Now arrange the circled letters to form the surprise answer, as suggested by the above cartoon.

Print answer here "[ ][ ][ ]! — & [ ][ ][ ][ ][ ][ ]"

PUZZLE
135

JUMBLE®

Unscramble these four Jumbles, one letter to each square, to form four ordinary words.

FLEAY

NUFTO

WRALEY

LOSTID

C'mon—get with it!

WHAT THE GEOLOGIST WHO SPECIALIZED IN EARTHQUAKES WAS.

Now arrange the circled letters to form the surprise answer, as suggested by the above cartoon.

Print answer here A " "

PUZZLE
136

JUMBLE®

Unscramble these four Jumbles, one letter to each square, to form four ordinary words.

LINAF
YUDAG
REHITE
UCCSAU
Hmph!
THE ONLY THING A PESSIMIST EVER EXPECTS ON A SILVER PLATTER.

Now arrange the circled letters to form the surprise answer, as suggested by the above cartoon.

Print answer here

PUZZLE
137

JUMBLE®

Unscramble these four Jumbles, one letter to each square, to form four ordinary words.

NOCIT
NUMOR
TUPPIL
ENCOAB
Doesn't waste time
HE BECAME MAN OF THE HOUR BECAUSE HE KNEW HOW TO MAKE THIS.

Now arrange the circled letters to form the surprise answer, as suggested by the above cartoon.

Print answer here EVERY

PUZZLE
138

JUMBLE®

Unscramble these four Jumbles, one letter to each square, to form four ordinary words.

YOANG
RAWEY
HALINE
DYNKIL
Yak yak yak yak
?
THE BORE WOULDN'T STOP TALKING UNTIL HIS FRIEND STARTED THIS.

Now arrange the circled letters to form the surprise answer, as suggested by the above cartoon.

Print answer here

PUZZLE
139

JUMBLE®

Unscramble these four Jumbles, one letter to each square, to form four ordinary words.

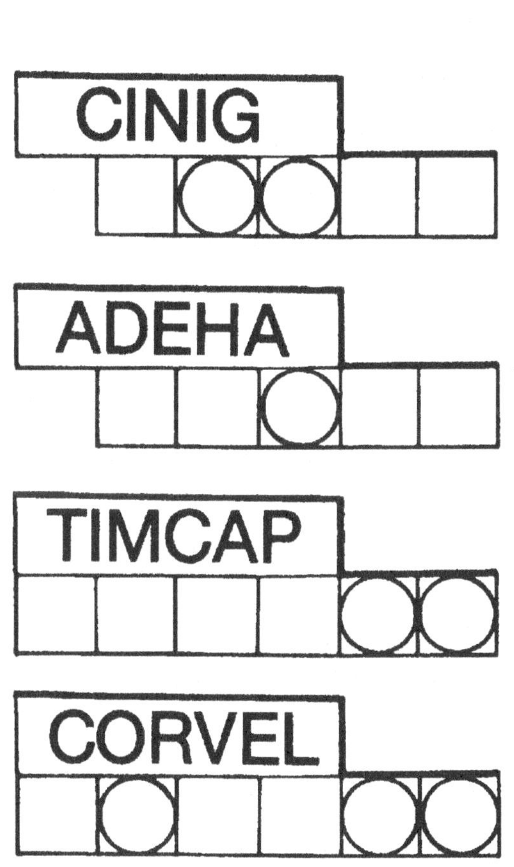
CINIG
ADEHA
TIMCAP
CORVEL

Must be some mistake
CHARGED WITH SOMETHING SHOCKING.

Now arrange the circled letters to form the surprise answer, as suggested by the above cartoon.

Print answer here

PUZZLE
140

JUMBLE®

Unscramble these four Jumbles, one letter to each square, to form four ordinary words.

YOWLL
LIRLT
HERNET
DINTUC
A SCRATCH PAD IS FOR PEOPLE WHO HAVE THIS AT ODD TIMES AND PLACES.

Now arrange the circled letters to form the surprise answer, as suggested by the above cartoon.

Print answer here THE ◯◯◯◯◯◯ TO ◯◯◯◯◯◯◯

PUZZLE
141

JUMBLE®

Unscramble these four Jumbles, one letter to each square, to form four ordinary words.

IFFYT

NAKTE

DAGNIE

BROBRE

WHAT THAT DEAFENING NOISE WAS A FORM OF.

Now arrange the circled letters to form the surprise answer, as suggested by the above cartoon.

Print answer here " ___ - _______ "

PUZZLE
142

JUMBLE®

Unscramble these four Jumbles, one letter to each square, to form four ordinary words.

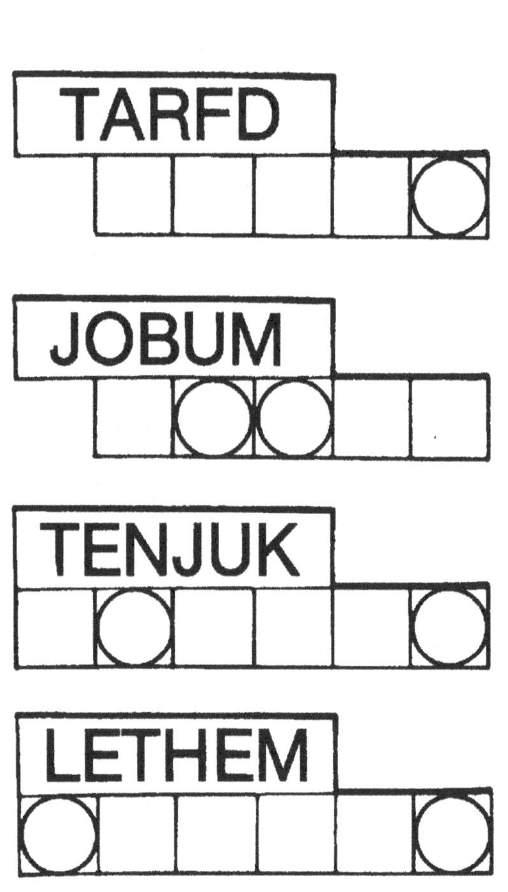
TARFD
JOBUM
TENJUK
LETHEM

WHAT A DOG HOUSE IS.

Now arrange the circled letters to form the surprise answer, as suggested by the above cartoon.

Print answer here A 

PUZZLE
143

JUMBLE®

Unscramble these four Jumbles, one letter to each square, to form four ordinary words.

VALGE
NALFK
SNODEC
DIMROB
DANCE
WHAT THE BOUNCER AT THAT COUNTRY AND WESTERN CLUB WAS.

Now arrange the circled letters to form the surprise answer, as suggested by the above cartoon.

Print answer here A " "

PUZZLE
144

JUMBLE®

Unscramble these four Jumbles, one letter to each square, to form four ordinary words.

KUFLE

DOORE

LIFFUT

BLABED

WHAT COFFEE OFTEN IS.

Now arrange the circled letters to form the surprise answer, as suggested by the above cartoon.

Print answer here A " "

PUZZLE
145

JUMBLE®

Unscramble these four Jumbles, one letter to each square, to form four ordinary words.

OGOIL
PHAMC
TABLLE
BIHRDY
AULD LANG SYNE
Good they're not driving tonight
WHAT NEW YEAR'S EVE MIGHT BE FOR SOME PEOPLE.
AN " "

Now arrange the circled letters to form the surprise answer, as suggested by the above cartoon.

PUZZLE
146

JUMBLE®

Unscramble these four Jumbles, one letter to each square, to form four ordinary words.

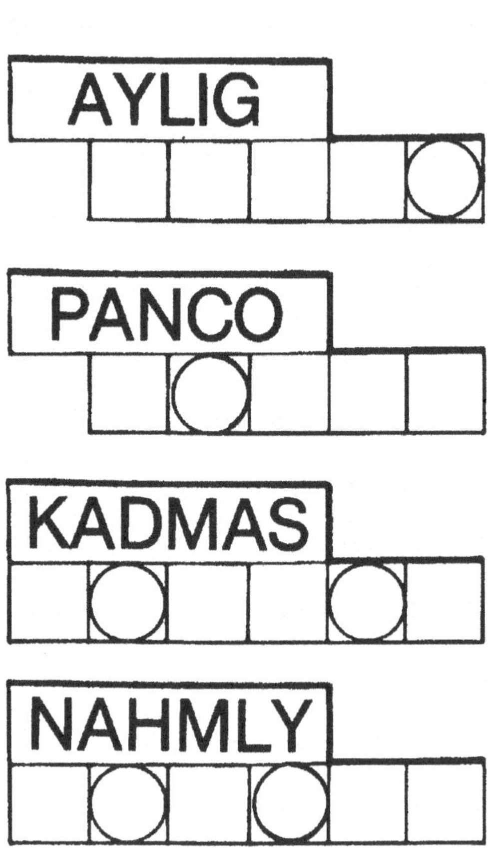
AYLIG
PANCO
KADMAS
NAHMLY

A GIRL WITH HORSE SENSE KNOWS WHEN TO DO THIS.

Now arrange the circled letters to form the surprise answer, as suggested by the above cartoon.

PUZZLE
147

JUMBLE®

Unscramble these four Jumbles, one letter to each square, to form four ordinary words.

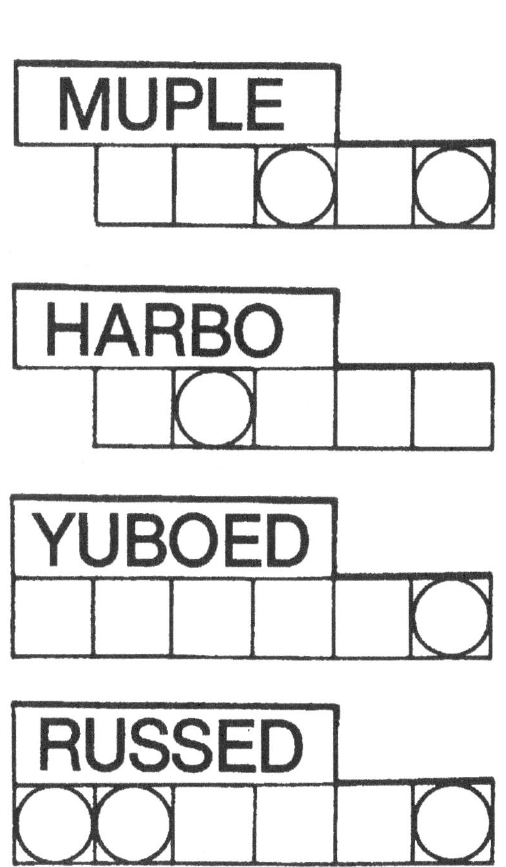
MUPLE
HARBO
YUBOED
RUSSED

WHAT THAT DUDE BECAME AFTER MARRIAGE.

Now arrange the circled letters to form the surprise answer, as suggested by the above cartoon.

Print answer here

PUZZLE
148

JUMBLE®

Unscramble these four Jumbles, one letter to each square, to form four ordinary words.

TULGI
OVEBA
THYROW
LURTIA
$ $
WHAT DOES A SMALL INLAY COST THESE DAYS?

Now arrange the circled letters to form the surprise answer, as suggested by the above cartoon.

Print answer here A

PUZZLE
149

JUMBLE®

Unscramble these four Jumbles, one letter to each square, to form four ordinary words.

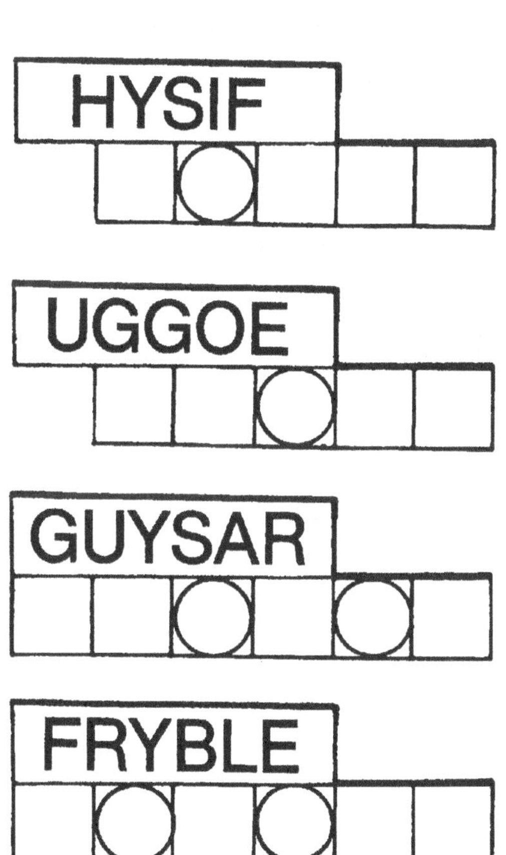
HYSIF
UGGOE
GUYSAR
FRYBLE

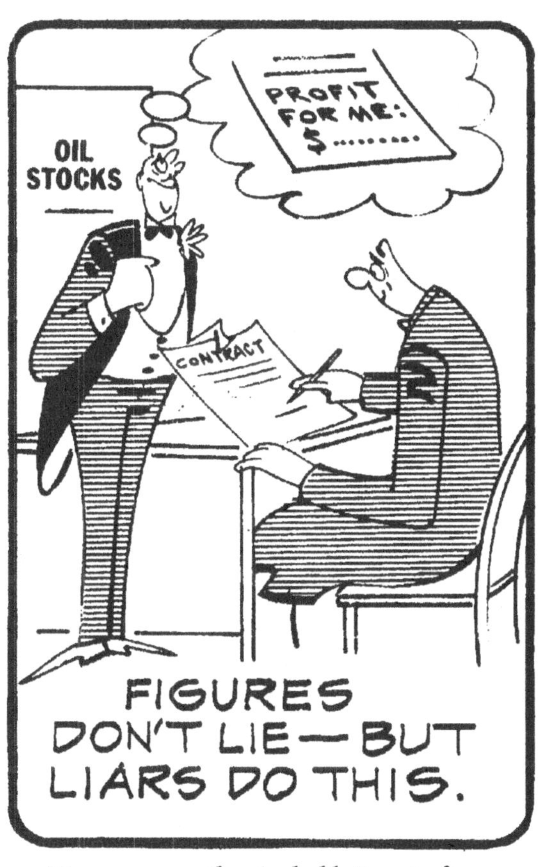
PROFIT FOR ME:
$........
OIL STOCKS
CONTRACT
FIGURES DON'T LIE—BUT LIARS DO THIS.

Now arrange the circled letters to form the surprise answer, as suggested by the above cartoon.

Print answer here 

PUZZLE
150

JUMBLE®

Unscramble these four Jumbles, one letter to each square, to form four ordinary words.

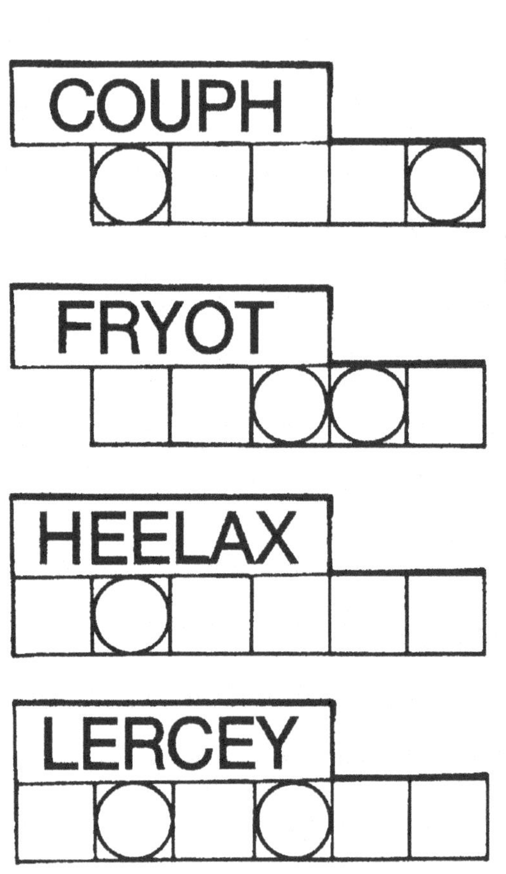

COUPH
FRYOT
HEELAX
LERCEY

When I cast spells they stay cast!
WHAT THAT SKILLFUL WITCH WAS.

Now arrange the circled letters to form the surprise answer, as suggested by the above cartoon.

Print answer here A "◯◯◯-◯◯◯◯◯"

PUZZLE
151

JUMBLE®

Unscramble these four Jumbles, one letter to each square, to form four ordinary words.

PLEEO

MOXIA

TOWWOK

CRYGLE

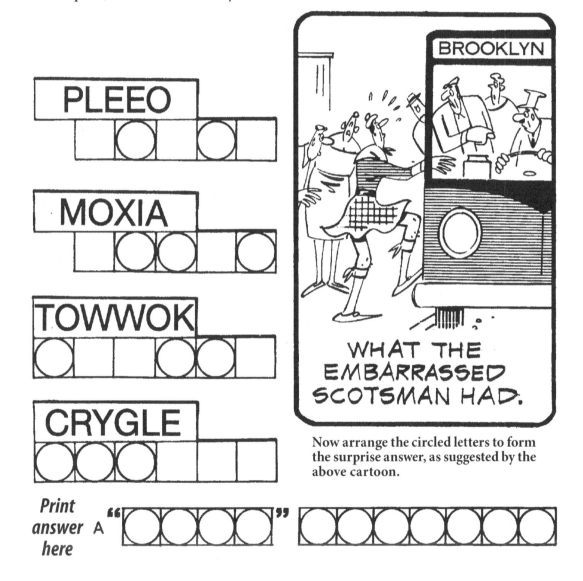

BROOKLYN

WHAT THE EMBARRASSED SCOTSMAN HAD.

Now arrange the circled letters to form the surprise answer, as suggested by the above cartoon.

Print answer here A " "

PUZZLE
152

JUMBLE®

Unscramble these four Jumbles, one letter to each square, to form four ordinary words.

TYFFI

WAQUS

THORUG

SEMIED

WHAT TANTRUMS IN CHILDHOOD APPEAR TO BE.

Now arrange the circled letters to form the surprise answer, as suggested by the above cartoon.

Print answer here THE " "

PUZZLE
153

JUMBLE®

Unscramble these four Jumbles, one letter to each square, to form four ordinary words.

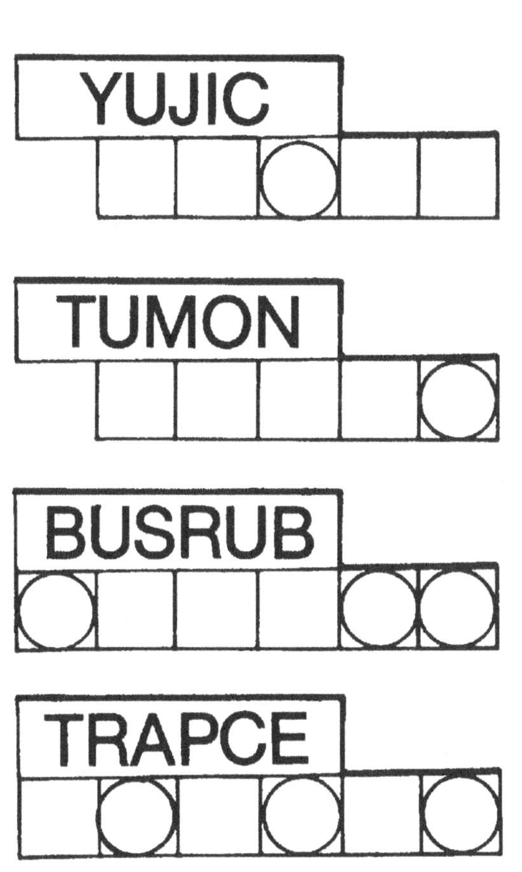
YUJIC
TUMON
BUSRUB
TRAPCE

Just you wait and see
WHAT DID THEY GIVE DRACULA WHEN HE FIRST WENT TO HOLLYWOOD?

Now arrange the circled letters to form the surprise answer, as suggested by the above cartoon.

Print answer here

PUZZLE
154

JUMBLE®
Unscramble these four Jumbles, one letter to each square, to form four ordinary words.
YOHBB
TOPIL
GIPNAY
FYLLAT
0000
WHAT'S A BALL HIT HIGH IN THE AIR DURING A GAME PLAYED AFTER DARK?
Now arrange the circled letters to form the surprise answer, as suggested by the above cartoon.
Print answer here
A

PUZZLE
155

JUMBLE®

Unscramble these four Jumbles, one letter to each square, to form four ordinary words.

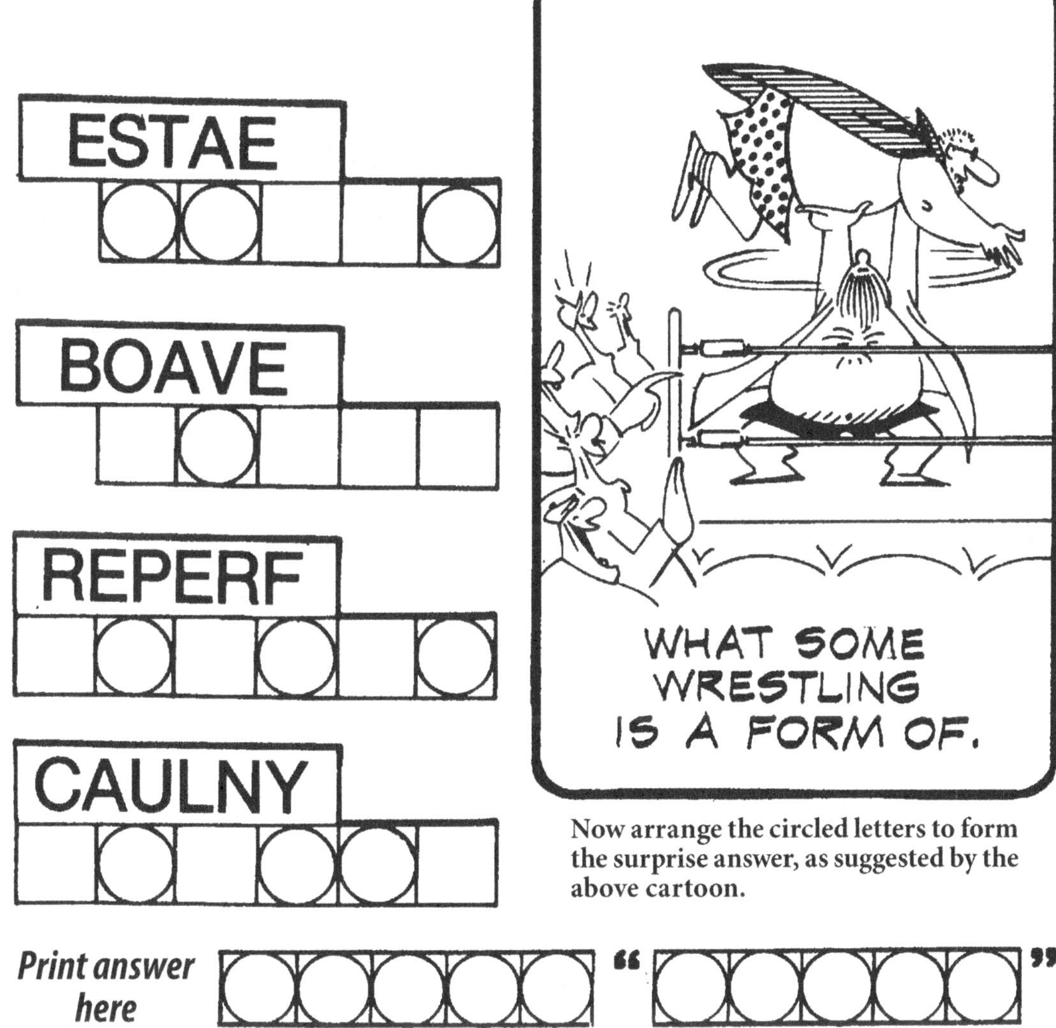
ESTAE
BOAVE
REPERF
CAULNY
WHAT SOME WRESTLING IS A FORM OF.
Now arrange the circled letters to form the surprise answer, as suggested by the above cartoon.
Print answer here
“ ”

PUZZLE
156

JUMBLE®

Unscramble these four Jumbles, one letter to each square, to form four ordinary words.

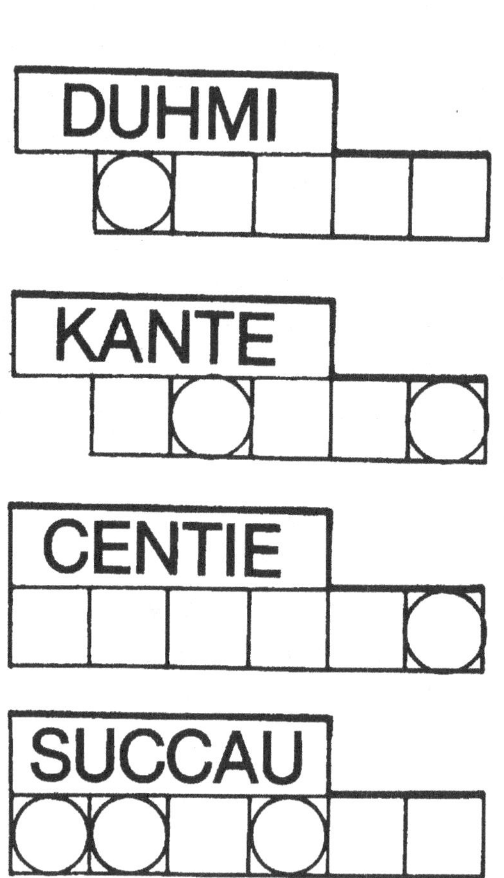
DUHMI
KANTE
CENTIE
SUCCAU

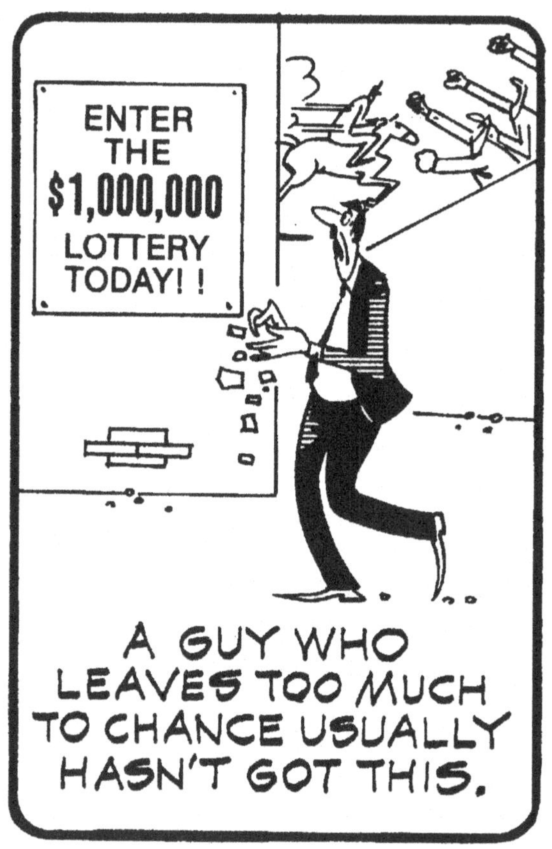
ENTER
THE
$1,000,000
LOTTERY
TODAY! !
A GUY WHO
LEAVES TOO MUCH
TO CHANCE USUALLY
HASN'T GOT THIS.

Now arrange the circled letters to form the surprise answer, as suggested by the above cartoon.

Print answer here

PUZZLE
157

JUMBLE®

Unscramble these four Jumbles, one letter to each square, to form four ordinary words.

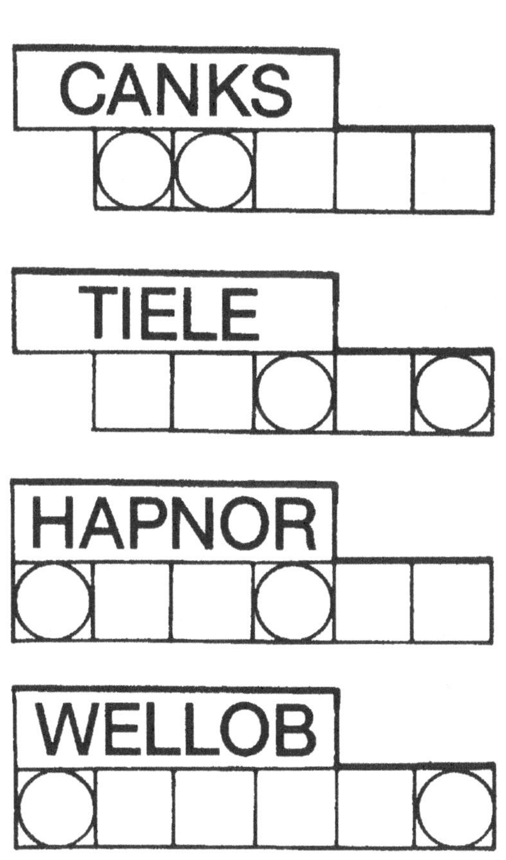
CANKS
TIELE
HAPNOR
WELLOB

SUCCESS IN LIFE OFTEN DEPENDS ON BACK-BONE, NOT THIS.

Now arrange the circled letters to form the surprise answer, as suggested by the above cartoon.

Print answer here

PUZZLE
158

JUMBLE®

Unscramble these four Jumbles, one letter to each square, to form four ordinary words.

CONIT

SUBGO

THROYP

DUMEGS

Whatever happened to trains?
Or bikes?
Or just plain walking?
WHAT MOST VACATIONERS SEEM TO BE THESE DAYS.

Now arrange the circled letters to form the surprise answer, as suggested by the above cartoon.

Print answer here " - - "

PUZZLE
159

JUMBLE®

Unscramble these four Jumbles, one letter to each square, to form four ordinary words.

LUGIE

TRAFE

DUBUSE

GLEGGI

Next she'll get her doctorate

HOW SHE IMPROVED HER KNOWLEDGE.

Now arrange the circled letters to form the surprise answer, as suggested by the above cartoon.

Print answer here BY

PUZZLE
160

JUMBLE®

Unscramble these four Jumbles, one letter to each square, to form four ordinary words.

ZEMIA
LORGY
YOCUTH
RAWSUL
WHAT THE OCTOPUS WORE TO THE FORMAL PARTY.

Now arrange the circled letters to form the surprise answer, as suggested by the above cartoon.

Print answer here A ◯◯◯◯ OF ◯◯◯◯

JUMBLE®

Gymnastics

Challenger Puzzles

PUZZLE
161

JUMBLE®

Unscramble these six Jumbles, one letter to each square, to form six ordinary words.

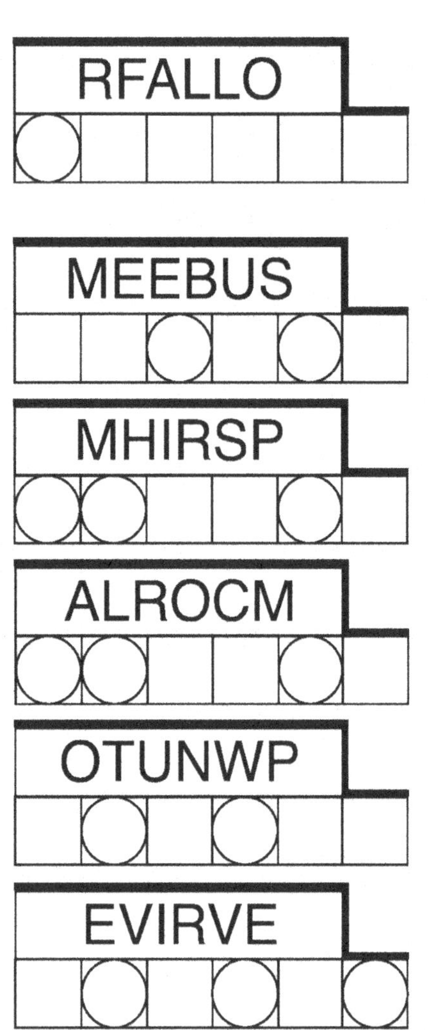

RFALLO
MEEBUS
MHIRSP
ALROCM
OTUNWP
EVIRVE

If you cough one more time, I quit!
AFTER LOSING HIS COOL DURING A PERFORMANCE, MOZART NEEDED TO DO THIS.

Now arrange the circled letters to form the surprise answer, as suggested by the above cartoon.

Print answer here

PUZZLE
162

JUMBLE®

Unscramble these six Jumbles, one letter to each square, to form six ordinary words.

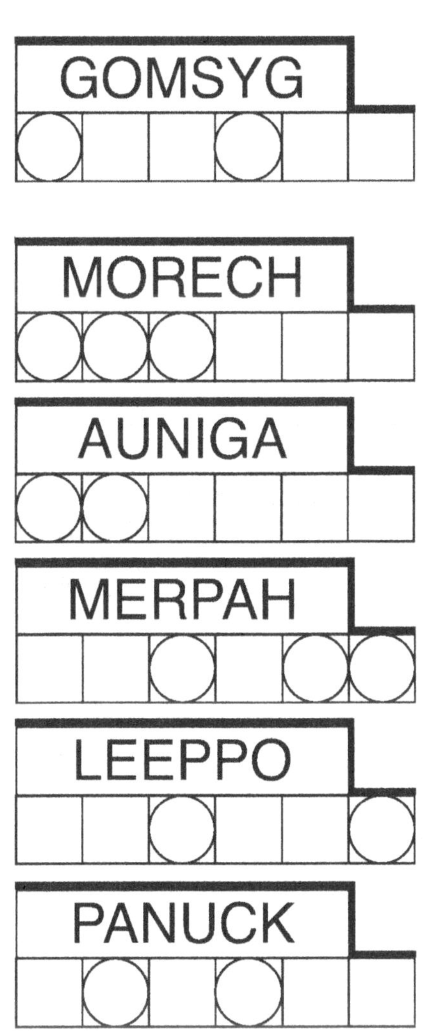
GOMSYG
MORECH
AUNIGA
MERPAH
LEEPPO
PANUCK

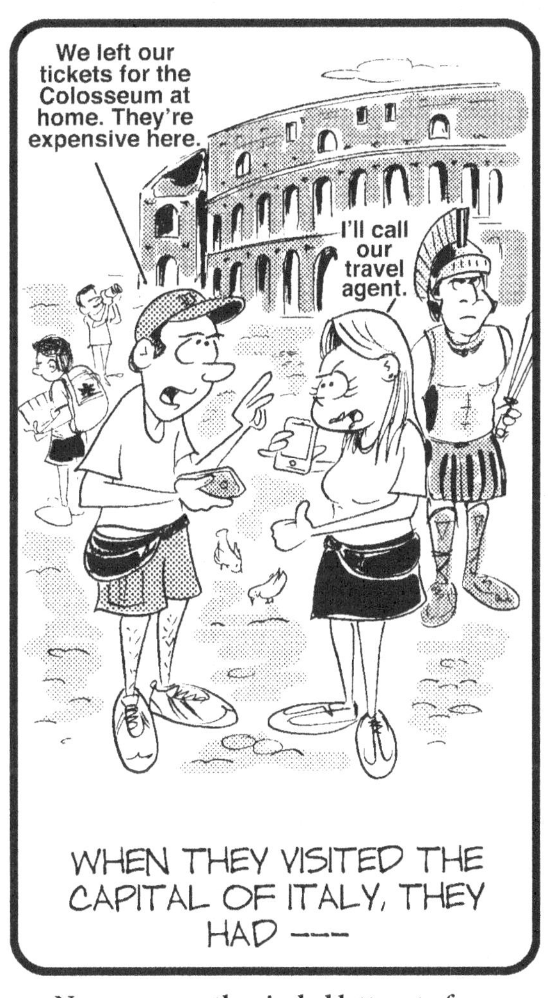
We left our tickets for the Colosseum at home. They're expensive here.
I'll call our travel agent.
WHEN THEY VISITED THE CAPITAL OF ITALY, THEY HAD ---

Now arrange the circled letters to form the surprise answer, as suggested by the above cartoon.

Print answer here

PUZZLE
163

JUMBLE®

Unscramble these six Jumbles, one letter to each square, to form six ordinary words.

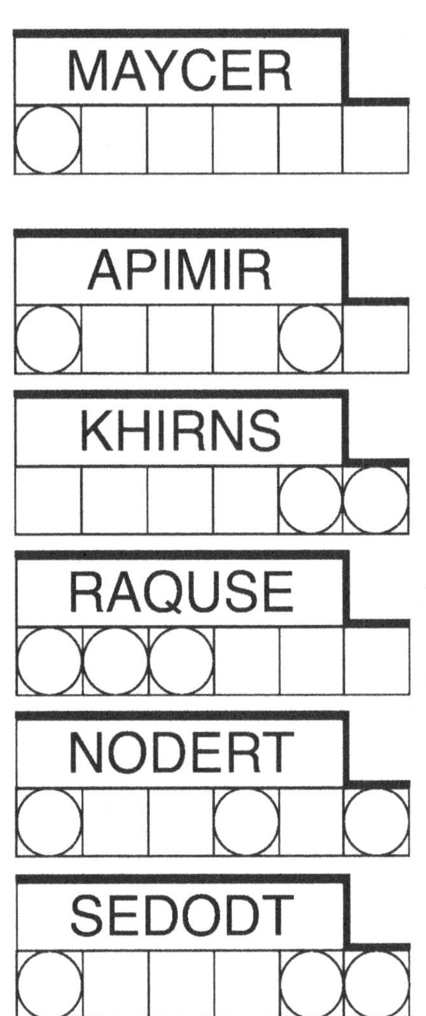
MAYCER
APIMIR
KHIRNS
RAQUSE
NODERT
SEDODT

MAC KING
COMEDY MAGIC
Do the cards scratch your wrist when they're up your sleeves? And how long can the goldfish stay alive in your pockets?
No. They just...Hey! Show's over. You have to leave.
THE MAGICIAN DIDN'T ANSWER BECAUSE HE DIDN'T LIKE THESE.

Now arrange the circled letters to form the surprise answer, as suggested by the above cartoon.

Print answer here

PUZZLE
164

JUMBLE®

Unscramble these six Jumbles, one letter to each square, to form six ordinary words.

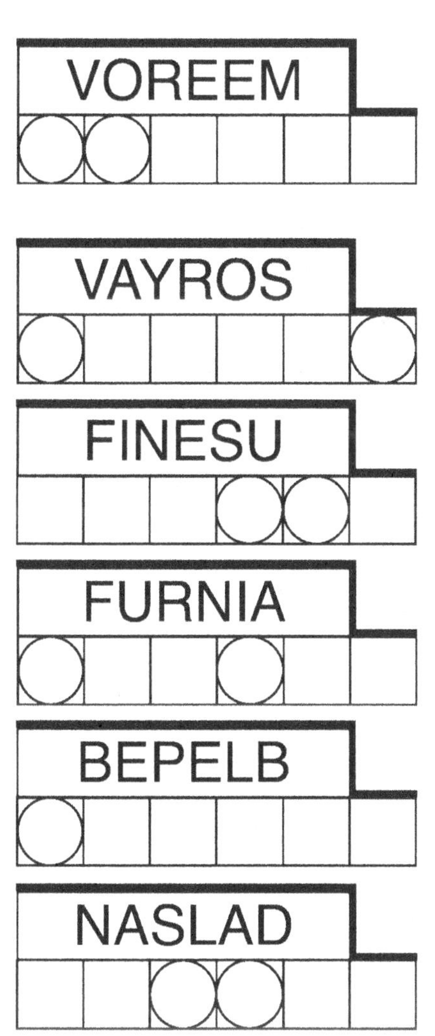

VOREEM
VAYROS
FINESU
FURNIA
BEPELB
NASLAD

XLVI
This is going to be great!
Awesome, baby!
WHEN THE AFC AND NFC MET IN THE CHAMPIONSHIP GAME, EVERYONE HAD A ---

Now arrange the circled letters to form the surprise answer, as suggested by the above cartoon.

Print answer here

PUZZLE
165

JUMBLE®

Unscramble these six Jumbles, one letter to each square, to form six ordinary words.

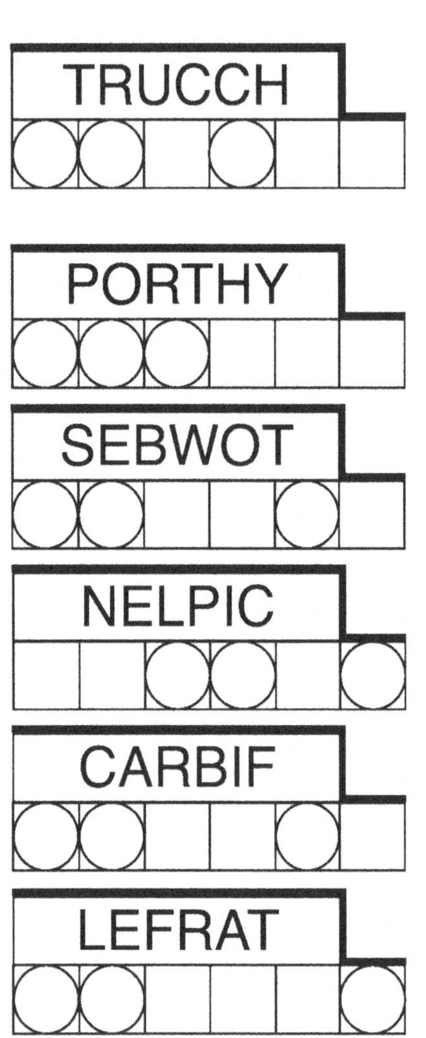
TRUCCH
PORTHY
SEBWOT
NELPIC
CARBIF
LEFRAT

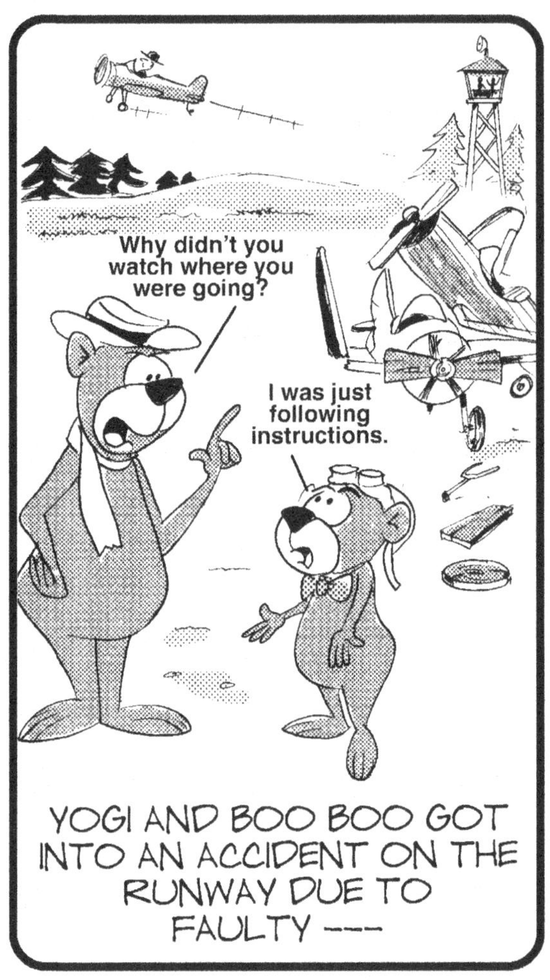
Why didn't you watch where you were going?
I was just following instructions.
YOGI AND BOO BOO GOT INTO AN ACCIDENT ON THE RUNWAY DUE TO FAULTY ---

Now arrange the circled letters to form the surprise answer, as suggested by the above cartoon.

Print answer here

PUZZLE
166

JUMBLE®

Unscramble these six Jumbles, one letter to each square, to form six ordinary words.

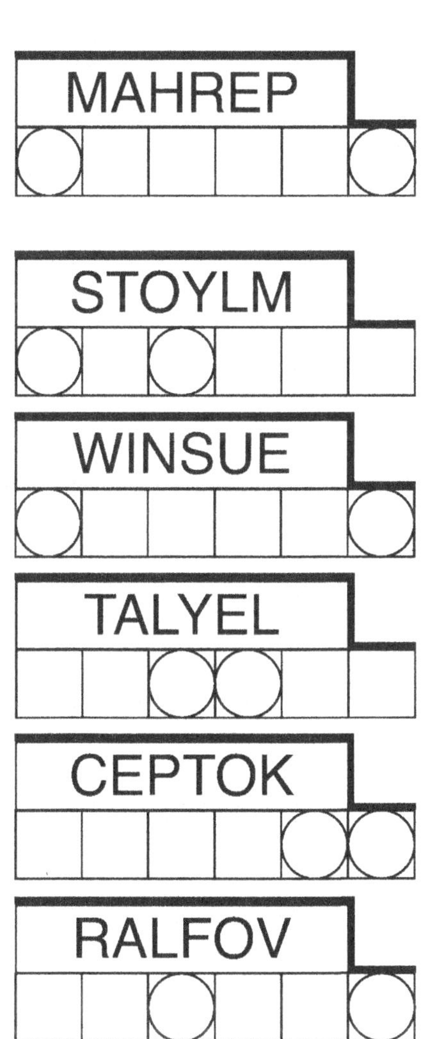
MAHREP
STOYLM
WINSUE
TALYEL
CEPTOK
RALFOV

These are my prized possessions ...I will never sell these after all the effort I put into finding them.
WHEN IT CAME TO THE GEMSTONES DATING BACK TO THE DAYS OF PIRATES, HE WOULD ---

Now arrange the circled letters to form the surprise answer, as suggested by the above cartoon.

Print answer here

PUZZLE
167

JUMBLE®

Unscramble these six Jumbles, one letter to each square, to form six ordinary words.

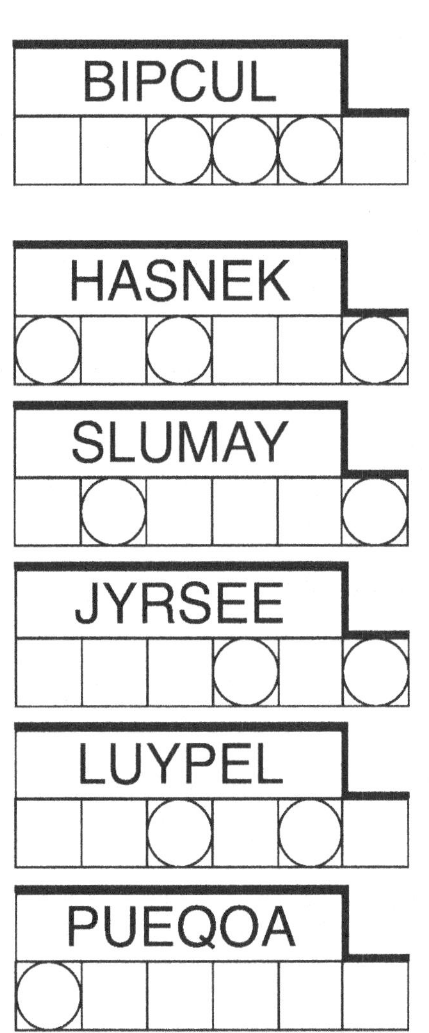
BIPCUL
HASNEK
SLUMAY
JYRSEE
LUYPEL
PUEQOA

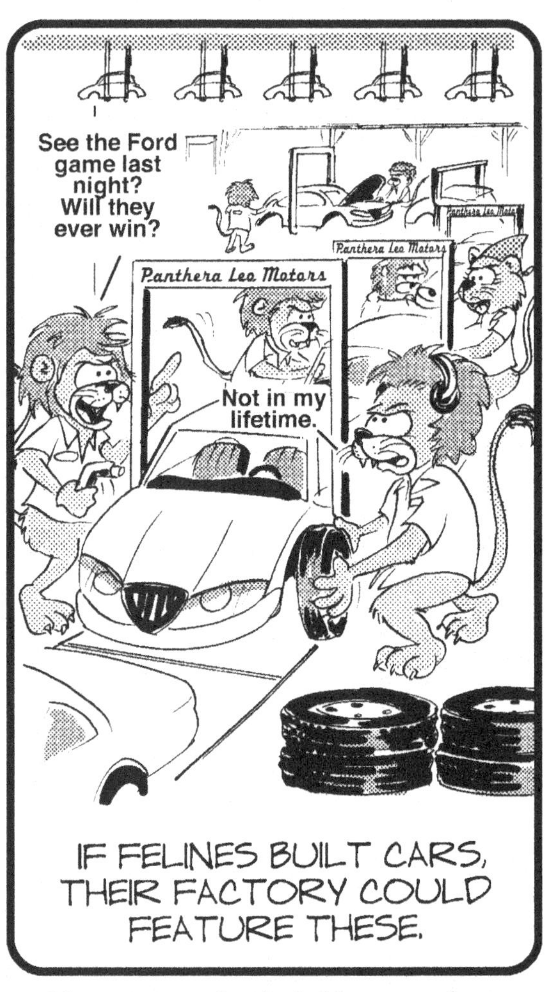
See the Ford game last night? Will they ever win?
Panthera Leo Motors
Not in my lifetime.
IF FELINES BUILT CARS, THEIR FACTORY COULD FEATURE THESE.

Now arrange the circled letters to form the surprise answer, as suggested by the above cartoon.

Print answer here

PUZZLE
168

JUMBLE®

Unscramble these six Jumbles, one letter to each square, to form six ordinary words.

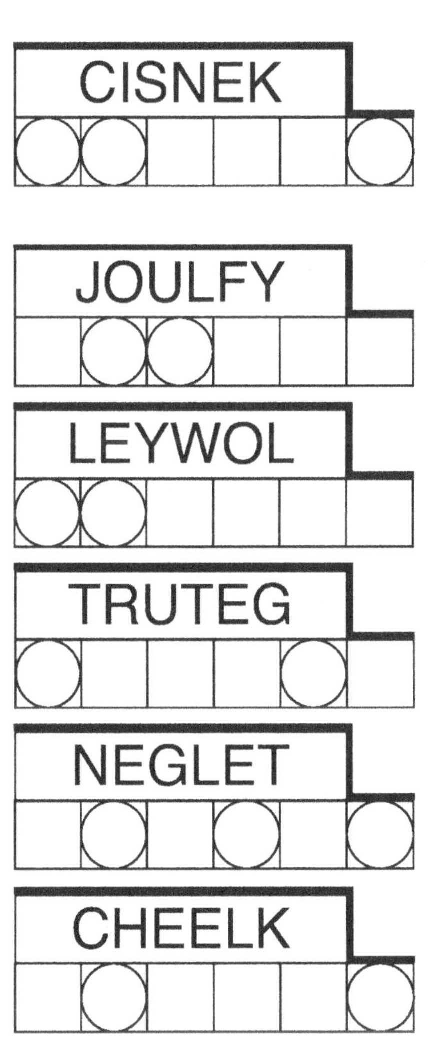

CISNEK
JOULFY
LEYWOL
TRUTEG
NEGLET
CHEELK

I'm stronger, so I'm going to club him first!
It's not fair! You always get to club them first.
THE CYCLOPES WEREN'T ---

Now arrange the circled letters to form the surprise answer, as suggested by the above cartoon.

Print answer here

PUZZLE
169

JUMBLE®

Unscramble these six Jumbles, one letter to each square, to form six ordinary words.

KIPSYM
NEAFIL
SWILEV
SULNES
FASRIA
RELNOL

I like this trail a lot. It sure is different.
I like the variety.
THE HIKING TRAIL HAD THIS ON IT.

Now arrange the circled letters to form the surprise answer, as suggested by the above cartoon.

Print answer here

PUZZLE
170

JUMBLE®

Unscramble these six Jumbles, one letter to each square, to form six ordinary words.

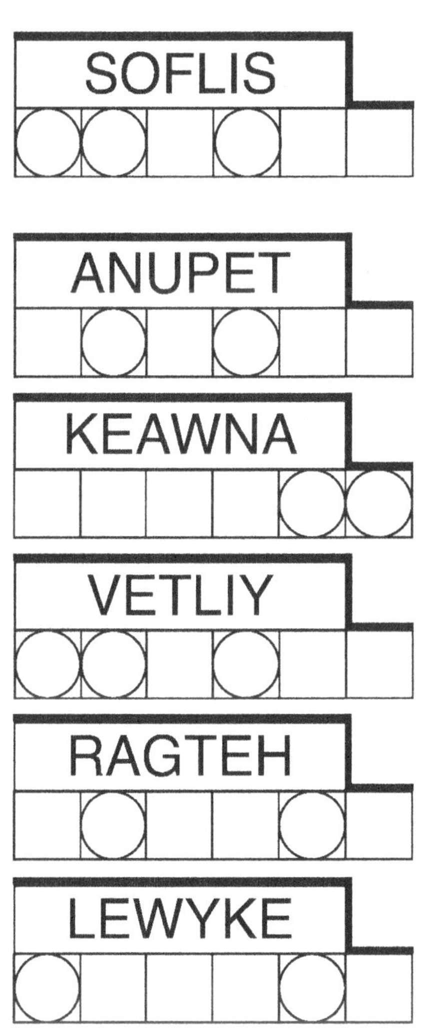
SOFLIS
ANUPET
KEAWNA
VETLIY
RAGTEH
LEWYKE

Thank you. This really helps me. I'm just getting over a bad breakup. I really need a fresh start.
That's nice, dear. Rent is due the first of the month.
RENTING THE APARTMENT WAS THIS FOR THE ZOMBIE.

Now arrange the circled letters to form the surprise answer, as suggested by the above cartoon.

Print answer here

A

PUZZLE
171

JUMBLE®

Unscramble these six Jumbles, one letter to each square, to form six ordinary words.

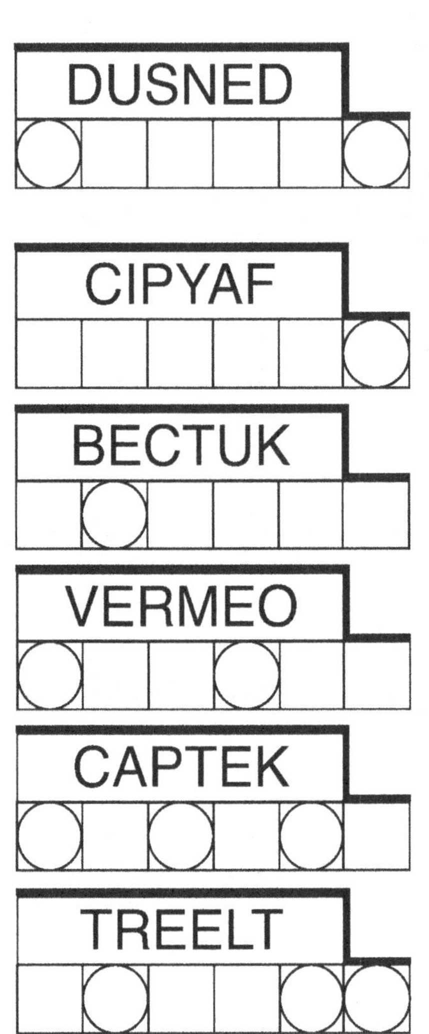
DUSNED
CIPYAF
BECTUK
VERMEO
CAPTEK
TREELT

We made stepping-stones, again!
I just love spending the day with you all! That's the best gift.
You have a whole path now.
CAM 2013
SYD 2013
CAM 2011
OF ALL THE GIFTS YOU GAVE YOUR MOM ON MOTHER'S DAY, HER FAVORITE HAS ALWAYS BEEN ---

Now arrange the circled letters to form the surprise answer, as suggested by the above cartoon.

Print answer here

PUZZLE
172

JUMBLE®

Unscramble these six Jumbles, one letter to each square, to form six ordinary words.

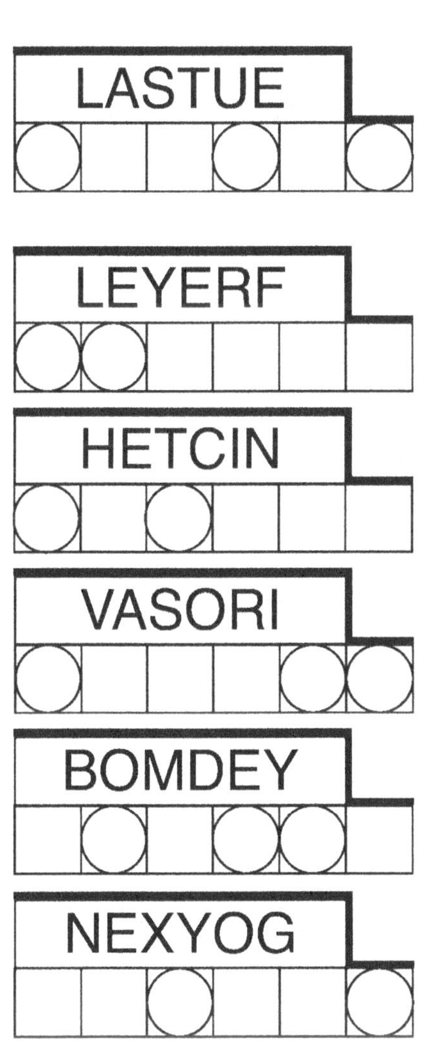
LASTUE
LEYERF
HETCIN
VASORI
BOMDEY
NEXYOG

The Mojave Chamber of Commerce Presents
DEATH VALLEY COMEDY JAM
I bought some dehydrated water, but I don't know what to add to it.
SOX
THE COMEDIAN AT THE DEATH VALLEY COMEDY FESTIVAL HAD A ---

Now arrange the circled letters to form the surprise answer, as suggested by the above cartoon.

Print answer here

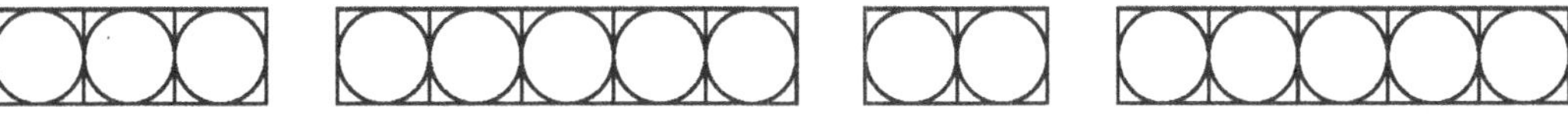

PUZZLE
173

JUMBLE®

Unscramble these six Jumbles, one letter to each square, to form six ordinary words.

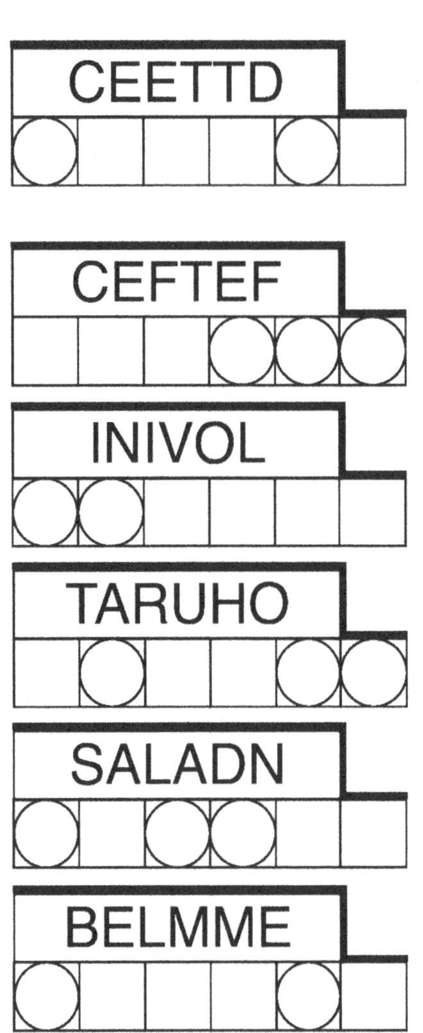
CEETTD
CEFTEF
INIVOL
TARUHO
SALADN
BELMME

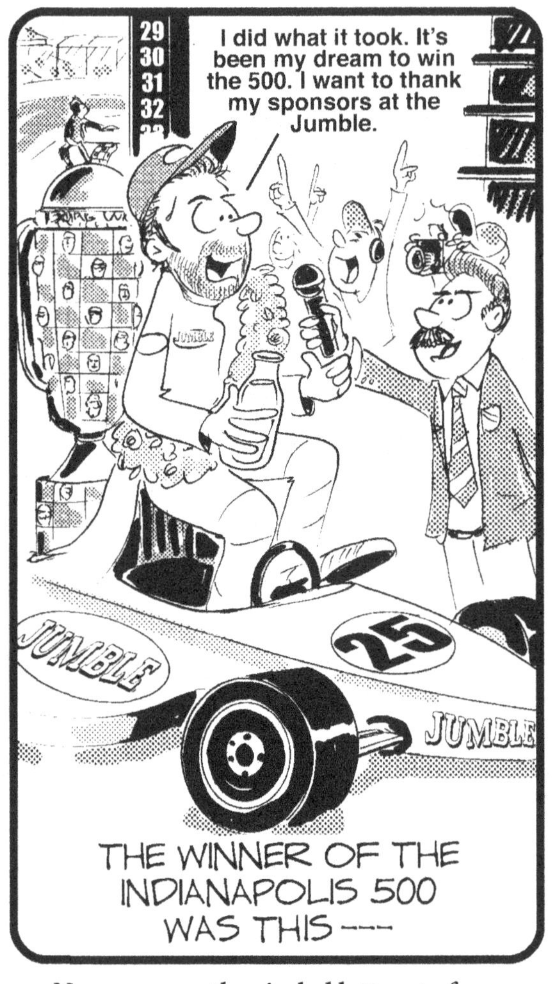
I did what it took. It's been my dream to win the 500. I want to thank my sponsors at the Jumble.
29
30
31
32
JUMBLE
25
JUMBLE

THE WINNER OF THE INDIANAPOLIS 500 WAS THIS ---

Now arrange the circled letters to form the surprise answer, as suggested by the above cartoon.

Print answer here

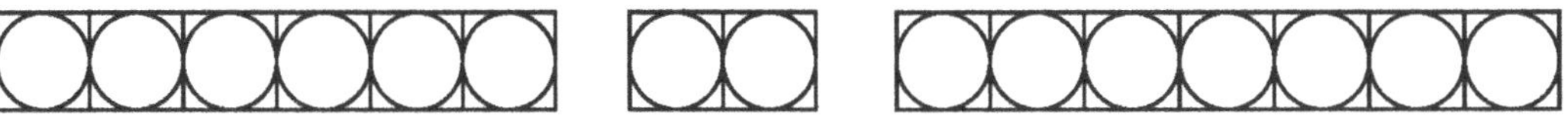

PUZZLE
174

JUMBLE®

Unscramble these six Jumbles, one letter to each square, to form six ordinary words.

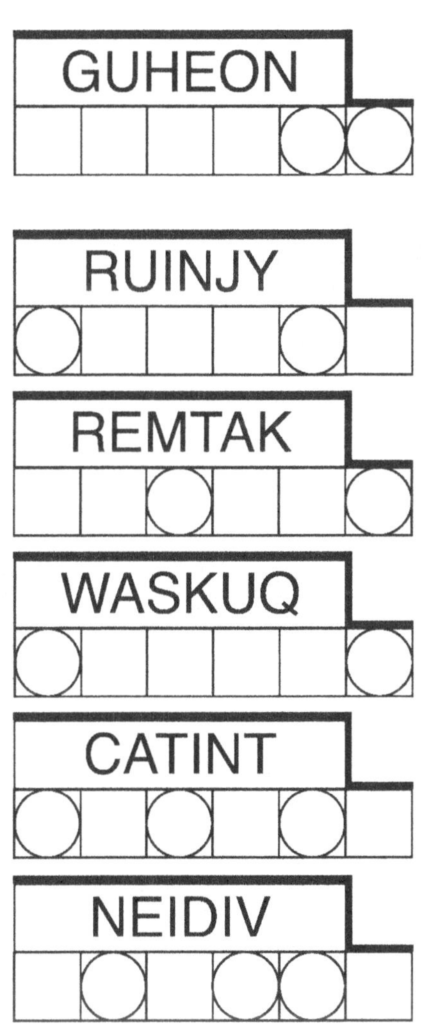
GUHEON
RUINJY
REMTAK
WASKUQ
CATINT
NEIDIV

McCracken X X X / X X X / / X /
Munson X X / X X / X X / X
You had better not leave any standing.
$1,000,000 Bowling Championship
Oh, they're all going down. That prize is mine.
HE ENTERED THE BOWLING TOURNAMENT IN THE HOPE OF ---

Now arrange the circled letters to form the surprise answer, as suggested by the above cartoon.

Print answer here

PUZZLE
175

JUMBLE®

Unscramble these six Jumbles, one letter to each square, to form six ordinary words.

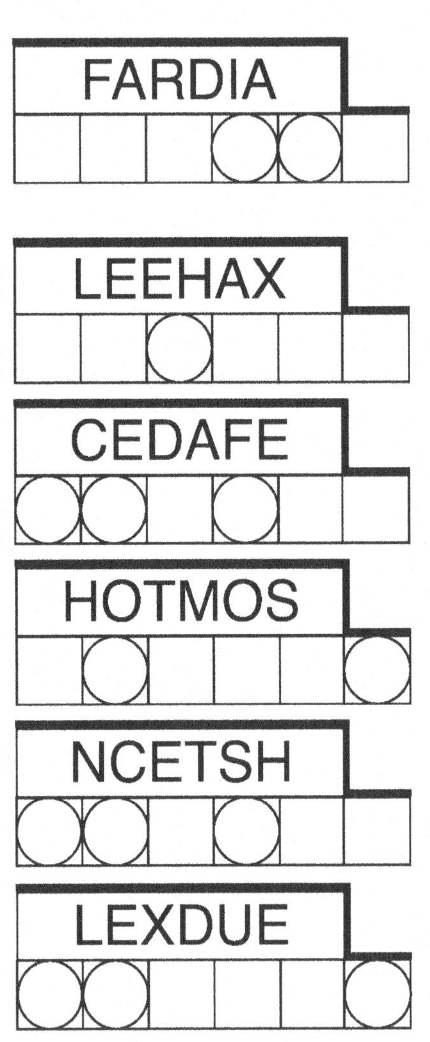

FARDIA
LEEHAX
CEDAFE
HOTMOS
NCETSH
LEXDUE

Wow, honey! This looks great!
It will be the perfect place to relax this summer.
AFTER BUILDING A NEW DECK UNDERNEATH THE LARGE OAK TREE, HE HAD IT ---

Now arrange the circled letters to form the surprise answer, as suggested by the above cartoon.

Print answer here

PUZZLE
176

JUMBLE®

Unscramble these six Jumbles, one letter to each square, to form six ordinary words.

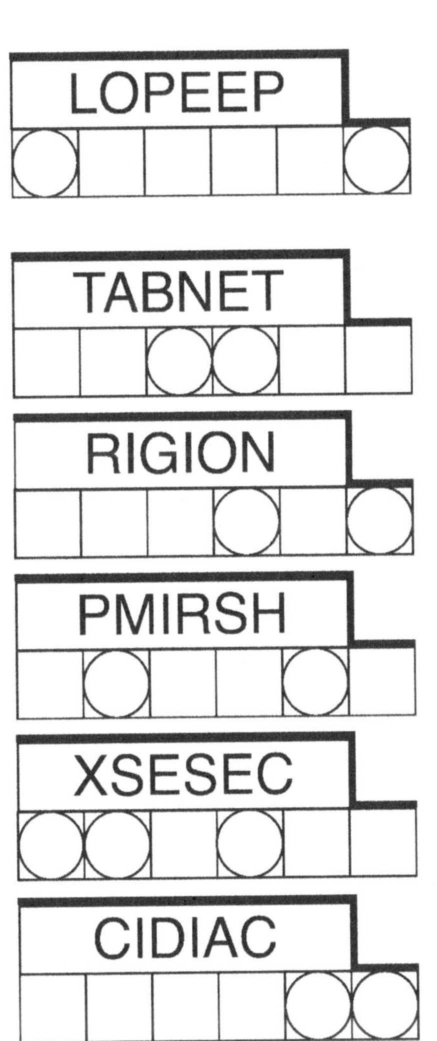
LOPEEP
TABNET
RIGION
PMIRSH
XSESEC
CIDIAC

Honey, I think the twins are telling me they're ready.
What? I'm not ready! What do we do?
SHE WASN'T SURPRISED WHEN HER LABOR PAINS BEGAN BECAUSE SHE WAS ---

Now arrange the circled letters to form the surprise answer, as suggested by the above cartoon.

Print answer here

PUZZLE
177

JUMBLE®

Unscramble these six Jumbles, one letter to each square, to form six ordinary words.

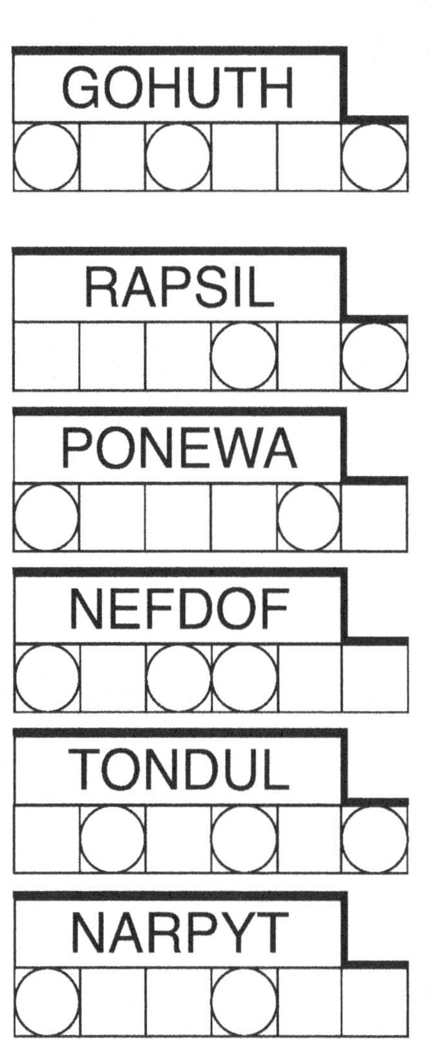
GOHUTH
RAPSIL
PONEWA
NEFDOF
TONDUL
NARPYT

We did it! I can't believe it.
I'll plant our flag right on the pole.
WHEN THE EXPLORERS REACHED THE NORTH POLE, THEY WERE ---

Now arrange the circled letters to form the surprise answer, as suggested by the above cartoon.

Print answer here

PUZZLE
178

JUMBLE®

Unscramble these six Jumbles, one letter to each square, to form six ordinary words.

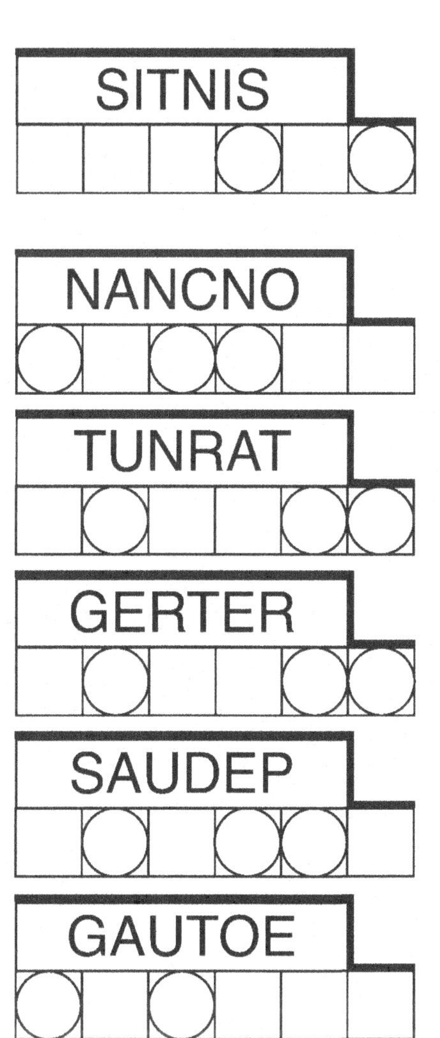
SITNIS
NANCNO
TUNRAT
GERTER
SAUDEP
GAUTOE

Look at that.
What's going on there?
Excuse me, sir. My dog is smelling something. I need to check.
ARRR
ARRR
K9 PATROL
ARRR
Oh, my
THE AIRPORT'S SECURITY CANINE WAS THE ---

Now arrange the circled letters to form the surprise answer, as suggested by the above cartoon.

Print answer here

" " OF

PUZZLE
179

JUMBLE®

Unscramble these six Jumbles, one letter to each square, to form six ordinary words.

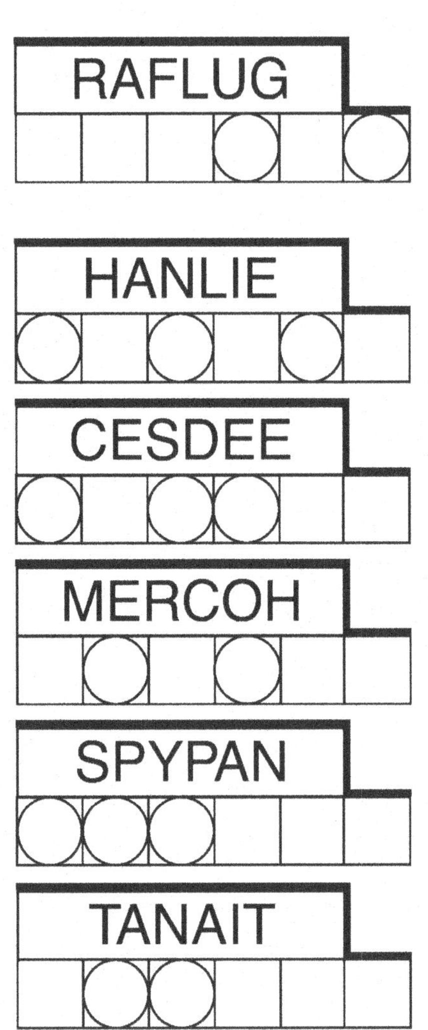
RAFLUG
HANLIE
CESDEE
MERCOH
SPYPAN
TANAIT

Take this 7 iron and hit it exactly 155 yards. Aim 30 yards left, because the wind is blowing in off the coast.
You had better listen to him.
THE GOLFER'S CADDIE WAS ---

Now arrange the circled letters to form the surprise answer, as suggested by the above cartoon.

Print answer here

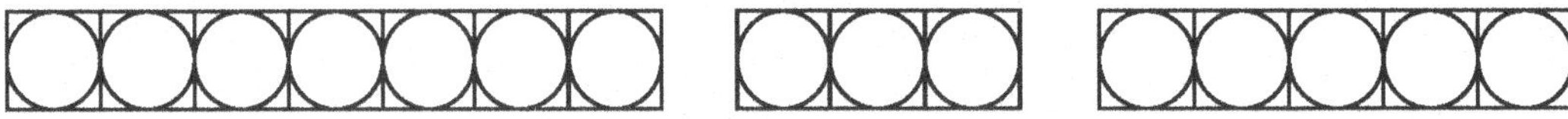

PUZZLE
180

JUMBLE®

Unscramble these six Jumbles, one letter to each square, to form six ordinary words.

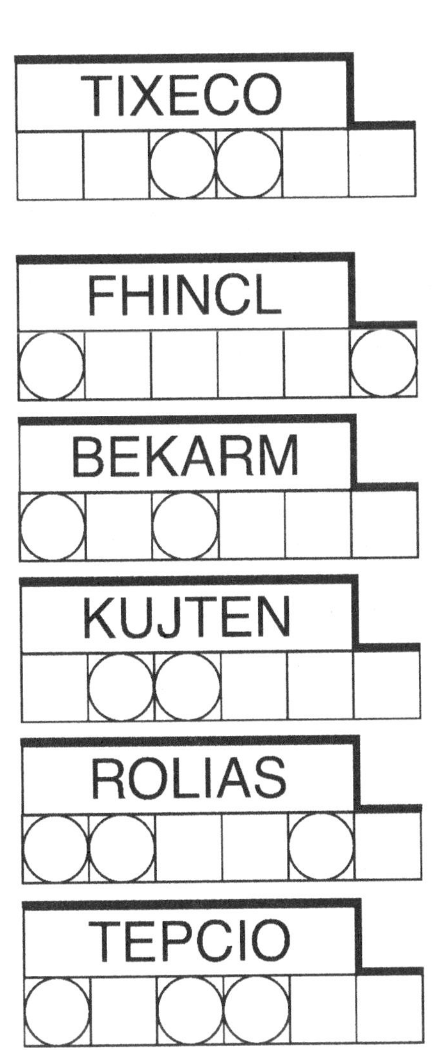
TIXECO
FHINCL
BEKARM
KUJTEN
ROLIAS
TEPCIO

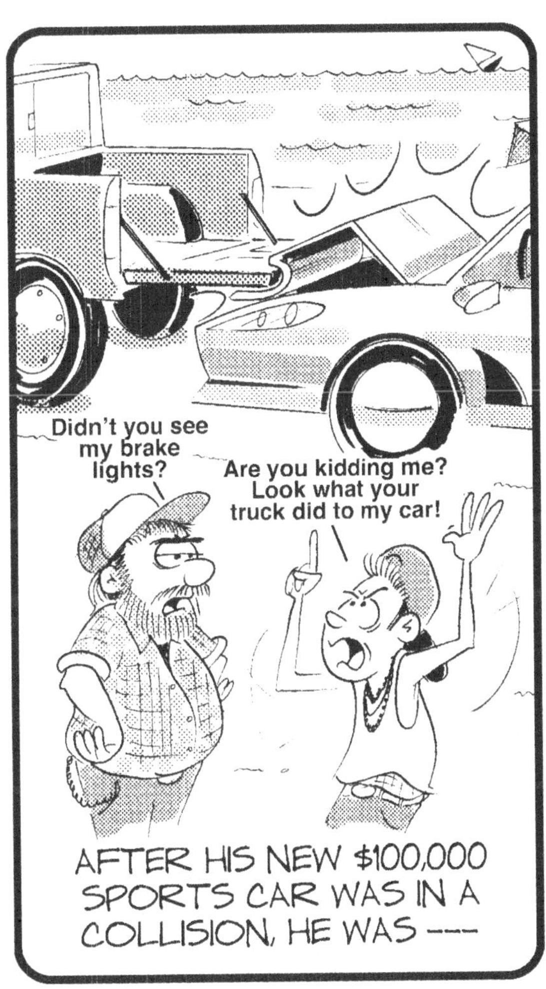
Didn't you see my brake lights?
Are you kidding me? Look what your truck did to my car!
AFTER HIS NEW $100,000 SPORTS CAR WAS IN A COLLISION, HE WAS ---

Now arrange the circled letters to form the surprise answer, as suggested by the above cartoon.

Print answer here

ANSWERS

1. **Jumbles:** OBESE NUDGE JOYFUL VELVET
Answer: What a cafeteria offers—"SEE" FOOD
2. **Jumbles:** PLAID SYNOD WHALER WAYLAY
Answer: What they considered the card shark's suggestion—A SHADY DEAL
3. **Jumbles:** HENCE BUILT GLOOMY LUNACY
Answer: What she was looking for at the singles dance—A MATCH
4. **Jumbles:** OZONE LOONY GUZZLE TOWARD
Answer: What the boss said when they struck oil—"WELL DONE"
5. **Jumbles:** CHESS LOUSE PEPTIC GAIETY
Answer: Pursuing the church thief resulted in this—A STEEPLE CHASE
6. **Jumbles:** GIANT GRAVE HERALD TEACUP
Answer: What the English decorator had—A CHANGE OF 'ART
7. **Jumbles:** DRAMA FUNNY STOLID BUZZER
Answer: When it came to commitment the confirmed bachelor was this—UNBRIDLED
8. **Jumbles:** FAVOR HAVEN VIRILE VORTEX
Answer: When the washing machine broke it left mom—IN A LATHER
9. **Jumbles:** MINUS AZURE RAMROD RUBBER
Answer: Corporate black moods can be caused by this—RED NUMBERS
10. **Jumbles:** GUILT MOOSE TIMING INJURY
Answer: What lawyers often face in a courtroom—TRYING TIMES
11. **Jumbles:** BOUND VYING WHITEN DEFILE
Answer: What the bettor wanted to do at the window—WIN DOUGH
12. **Jumbles:** FAITH PARKA UNSOLD ENJOIN
Answer: What the runner called the initial stop in the marathon—FIRST "ADE"
13. **Jumbles:** CEASE TRYST UNLIKE WISDOM
Answer: Breakfast jam on the morning paper can become this—A STICKY ISSUE
14. **Jumbles:** MONEY BROOK TRUDGE HAZARD
Answer: Successful road builders do this—MAKE THE GRADE
15. **Jumbles:** VENOM ARBOR DEADLY SUBURB
Answer: Where the hobos liked to rest—ON A ROAD "BED"
16. **Jumbles:** FLING GOING TWENTY BOLDLY
Answer: The owner of the toupee company was a—BIGWIG
17. **Jumbles:** FLANK ABATE FAÇADE TURNIP
Answer: Leonard Nimoy's career really took off as a result of him being—"ALIEN-ATED"
18. **Jumbles:** VIRUS DECAY FOURTH HEALTH
Answer: He didn't get the joke about the ceiling because it was—OVER HIS HEAD
19. **Jumbles:** ONION STASH COUPLE COUGAR
Answer: When they counted the prisoners, the result was a—"CON-CENSUS"
20. **Jumbles:** FORCE SPURN TOMATO MINGLE
Answer: Forrest Gump's shrimp business resulted in—NET PROFITS
21. **Jumbles:** TINGE TIPSY TANDEM FORMAL
Answer: The insect was no longer bugging him, and was quickly becoming his—"PEST" FRIEND
22. **Jumbles:** GRANT GOURD STOCKY ZENITH
Answer: He arrested the painter because he was a—CON ARTIST
23. **Jumbles:** YIELD HITCH AFRAID STIGMA
Answer: After the thief was caught stealing the batteries, he was—CHARGED
24. **Jumbles:** AWFUL KNELT CRANKY AGENDA
Answer: After fleeing into the laundromat, the suspect had no chance of a—CLEAN GETAWAY
25. **Jumbles:** HONEY PIVOT REMOVE GENIUS
Answer: After tracking down the stolen brooch, he had all the evidence he needed to—PIN IT ON HER
26. **Jumbles:** CLICK FRAME SICKLY BRIGHT
Answer: The Rebel bowling team was leading, but players worried the Empire's team might—STRIKE BACK
27. **Jumbles:** ALOUD BOOTH TRIPLE SHRINK
Answer: Something was wrong with the telescope, he would need to—LOOK INTO IT
28. **Jumbles:** VAULT CLERK LESSON CANDID
Answer: The food was pretty good at the skunk restaurant, but the—SERVICE STUNK
29. **Jumbles:** SILKY HEAVY SIDING FALLEN
Answer: She would apply coats of varnish until the table was—FINISHED
30. **Jumbles:** ADAPT VIGIL DRENCH WEASEL
Answer: The zombie bride was hard to carry over the threshold because she was—DEAD WEIGHT
31. **Jumbles:** VENOM STALL ETHNIC UNJUST
Answer: The guest's rude comments about the lodging establishment were—"INN-SULTS"
32. **Jumbles:** BLANK ABATE SCORCH PICKLE
Answer: In order to lose weight, the overeater would need to—SCALE BACK
33. **Jumbles:** TRACK AMUSE LEEWAY UNPAID
Answer: The guests at the lion's birthday celebration were—PARTY ANIMALS
34. **Jumbles:** SWORN PERCH AUTUMN ABSORB
Answer: When it came to his twin boys, there was no—"COMPARE-A-SON"
35. **Jumbles:** FRESH CLOCK INFLUX DETACH
Answer: He thought the telemarketer's interruption was—UNCALLED FOR
36. **Jumbles:** AHEAD FLOOR TAVERN SHRILL
Answer: When they split the cost of the taxi ride, everyone paid his—"FARE" SHARE
37. **Jumbles:** BEIGE CHUMP PIGEON PURSUE
Answer: Their trip to the Christmas tree farm turned into a—"CHOPPING" SPREE
38. **Jumbles:** EVENT ABYSS MISFIT VIABLE
Answer: Declining their offer to join the poker game would be his—BEST BET
39. **Jumbles:** MIMIC SLASH DEVICE PHOBIA
Answer: The astronaut volunteered for the spacewalk because she wanted—SOME SPACE
40. **Jumbles:** TALLY RIGOR MEMBER SQUISH
Answer: They climbed the hill to see the sun come up because they were—EARLY RISERS
41. **Jumbles:** PARKA SWIFT MAGNET CLOSET
Answer: The Christmas costume brought out their cat's—SANTA "CLAWS"
42. **Jumbles:** PRIMP MACAW SWAYED LONELY
Answer: After he invented the Franklin stove, Ben was able to give people a—WARM WELCOME
43. **Jumbles:** AMAZE APRON SULFUR PURITY
Answer: What can you find in "Manila" that you can't find in "Tokyo"?—ANIMAL

44. **Jumbles:** ANKLE CLING PARISH TUXEDO
Answer: When they decided to name their island "Britain," everyone thought it was—A GREAT IDEA

45. **Jumbles:** PRICE VALET SOOTHE PHOBIA
Answer: Sometimes, changing in the locker room is—THE PITS

46. **Jumbles:** APRON TWICE LESSON HICCUP
Answer: The campers were interested in a new tent, so he gave them a—SALES PITCH

47. **Jumbles:** HIKER CLERK SPOTTY LEEWAY
Answer: After getting into a traffic accident with his wife's car, he was a—TOTAL WRECK

48. **Jumbles:** YOUTH IMPEL ABACUS DECADE
Answer: The pizza parlor's approach to getting customers to make a purchase was—"BUY" THE SLICE

49. **Jumbles:** GIANT BOOTH VIABLE AUBURN
Answer: The documentary about the construction of the Eifel Tower was—RIVETING

50. **Jumbles:** BLURT PERCH NOVICE BLOTCH
Answer: The St. Patrick's Day scam artist was attempting a—"LEPRE-CON"

51. **Jumbles:** FLIRT ISSUE JACKET NOODLE
Answer: To print out the page with the Boeing 747 on it, he used—AN INK JET

52. **Jumbles:** NIECE FRAUD ISLAND EMERGE
Answer: He didn't think he would be eaten by a crocodile, but he was—IN "DE-NILE"

53. **Jumbles:** ORBIT VENOM SICKEN FRUGAL
Answer: The cemetery raised its burial fees and blamed in on the—COST OF LIVING

54. **Jumbles:** AROSE OFTEN STIGMA UNSAID
Answer: The former male model's calendar photos were—OUT-OF-DATE

55. **Jumbles:** STOOD THEFT SWATCH APIECE
Answer: The Dalmatian said this to the masseuse during her massage—THAT'S THE SPOT

56. **Jumbles:** ICILY MEALY EITHER SQUALL
Answer: What the bowling team called their mascot—AN "ALLEY" CAT

57. **Jumbles:** IRONY BUMPY HANGAR WISELY
Answer: What she kept getting on her phone bill—WRONG NUMBERS

58. **Jumbles:** HEAVY PIVOT UNLESS ZENITH
Answer: How the herder felt when he lost his flock—SHEEPISH

59. **Jumbles:** TONIC SUAVE FINITE SNUGLY
Answer: Why he bought her perfume—HE WAS SCENT-SITIVE

60. **Jumbles:** SKULK EMBER TRIBAL ACCENT
Answer: What the team called their annual dance—THE BASKET "BALL"

61. **Jumbles:** SEIZE FUSSY ENGULF REVERE
Answer: What overloaded trash collectors do—REFUSE REFUSE

62. **Jumbles:** SANDY COCOA COLUMN SATIRE
Answer: How the law students expressed their displeasure—WITH A "CLASS" ACTION

63. **Jumbles:** LIMBO EXACT YEARLY EMPIRE
Answer: What the actor's handyman role made him feel like—A BIT PLAYER

64. **Jumbles:** PLAIT TRULY BESIDE LOCATE
Answer: What a hotel room upgrade can become—A SUITE DEAL

65. **Jumbles:** FEWER SUITE EYELET PALLID
Answer: What the summons for jury duty is considered—THE LETTER OF THE LAW

66. **Jumbles:** TOXIN LIGHT TANKER HAGGLE
Answer: What the new lumberjacks seek that the others dread—GETTING THE AX

67. **Jumbles:** TEASE FLANK FLIMSY GOSPEL
Answer: How the shoemakers described themselves—"SOLE" MATES

68. **Jumbles:** FLOOR TABOO CENSUS BEHELD
Answer: Why the tired party-goer wanted to leave—SHE WAS BASH-FULL

69. **Jumbles:** CRIME JUMBO KIMONO FIASCO
Answer: What he loved most on the radio—"ROCK" MUSIC

70. **Jumbles:** JOLLY TEMPO DIVERT PALACE
Answer: What she considered her dog's obedience training—HER PET PROJECT

71. **Jumbles:** PENCE MAGIC BUSILY FIERCE
Answer: What he offered the prospective buyer—A "SAIL" PRICE

72. **Jumbles:** BEIGE PIKER FABRIC FACTOR
Answer: How she described her morning in rush hour—COFFEE, BREAK

73. **Jumbles:** POISE PUPPY EQUITY CLUMSY
Answer: What the barber was noted for—HIS "CLIP QUIPS"

74. **Jumbles:** BILGE TRACT CLOUDY UNWISE
Answer: How the frugal shopper made her purchasing decisions—"CENTS'-IBLY"

75. **Jumbles:** BELIE NATAL BEMOAN SEETHE
Answer: When the scoundrel danced with the ballerina it was—HEEL TO TOE

76. **Jumbles:** CROWN STOIC BEGONE LEDGER
Answer: What the shipwrecked crew called the bird's visit—A "GOOD TERN"

77. **Jumbles:** GAVEL TUNED COSTLY RANCID
Answer: What the coach gave the channel swimmers—"SOUND" ADVICE

78. **Jumbles:** TANGY ELATE BECALM LEEWAY
Answer: What the Australian wife called her tardy husband—HER LATE MATE

79. **Jumbles:** HIKER LUSTY BODICE SCURVY
Answer: What the rural visitor found in the urban store—A CITY SLICKER

80. **Jumbles:** DICED CAKED CALLOW TURBAN
Answer: How she succeeded on her diet—SHE BUCKLED DOWN

81. **Jumbles:** DEMON PUTTY HELIUM SIZZLE
Answer: He never fought with his wife because she knew how to—DISH IT OUT

82. **Jumbles:** STOKE SCOUT CHALET CORNER
Answer: What the electrician said the movie was—A REAL SHOCKER

83. **Jumbles:** JEWEL BRASS SCARCE ELICIT
Answer: What the writer on exotic wines was known for having—THE "BEST CELLAR"

84. **Jumbles:** CYNIC NERVY CALICO ENGINE
Answer: Another name for restoring a broken bike—RECYCLING

85. **Jumbles:** GORGE SNACK COWARD TRYING
Answer: What the contestants called the cooking contest—A "RANGE" WAR

86. **Jumbles:** ENSUE PEACE ATTACH VICUNA
Answer: What the crotchety doctor lacked—"PATIENTS"

87. **Jumbles:** FLOOD OWING HOMING STUDIO
Answer: Abe Lincoln's success was fueled by this—MIDNIGHT OIL

88. **Jumbles:** VIRUS DERBY BUTANE NUTRIA
Answer: Another name for an altar—A RITE SITE

89. **Jumbles:** KINKY TWINE JOSTLE PAROLE
Answer: Why the drama teacher became a coach—HE KNEW THE "PLAYS"

90. **Jumbles:** SHOWY CHICK LEAVEN GARISH
Answer: How the hot dog vendor handled his job—WITH "RELISH"

91. **Jumbles:** BLOOM BAGGY MOHAIR FLEECE
Answer: Combine classical and popular music and you get this—BACH AND ROLL

92. **Jumbles:** RIVET PIANO OXYGEN NAUSEA
Answer: What she thought of her clean bill of health—"EXPENSIVE"

93. **Jumbles:** DRAWL GLOVE BONNET INTAKE
Answer: That charming movie star was as likable as she was this—"LOOKABLE"

94. **Jumbles:** SUMAC PIOUS KIMONO PLENTY
Answer: What a good guitarist might have—EASY "PICKIN'S"

95. **Jumbles:** PUPPY CUBIT BEFALL MIDDAY
Answer: The latest thing out—THE BED LAMP

96. **Jumbles:** BULGY PAUSE MAROON SHREWD
Answer: How ballet has grown in popularity in recent years—BY LEAPS & BOUNDS

97. **Jumbles:** CRAFT LIMBO SINGLE BRIDLE
Answer: What a counterfeiter turned politician might be expected to pass—BAD BILLS

98. **Jumbles:** CHAFF GAILY SALOON HELPER
Answer: Another form of verbal abuse—"LIP LASH"

99. **Jumbles:** WHINE FEIGN DECENT OUTWIT
Answer: A banana skin may help to bring this—YOUR WEIGHT DOWN

100. **Jumbles:** GAMUT AFIRE SLOUCH EASILY
Answer: What their efforts at stealing apples were—FRUITLESS

101. **Jumbles:** COVEY MUSIC BAKERY INDOOR
Answer: What they said about the society girl the first time she appeared on TV—"DEB-ON-AIR"

102. **Jumbles:** BANJO HEFTY JACKAL SIZZLE
Answer: What a coward might do when he gets into a "jam"—SHAKE LIKE JELLY

103. **Jumbles:** NAVAL FEINT TURBAN LOCATE
Answer: What the confirmed bachelor's views were—"UN-ALTER-ABLE"

104. **Jumbles:** BEFIT OWING SPORTY ACCORD
Answer: Regardless of what the orchestra performs, the bass player has to do this—STAND FOR IT

105. **Jumbles:** KHAKI ABBEY JOCUND SLEIGH
Answer: An acrobat is the only person who can talk about himself this way—BEHIND HIS OWN BACK

106. **Jumbles:** GRAIN DADDY BUOYED MULISH
Answer: Why the crook disguised himself as a shepherd—HE WAS ON THE "LAMB"

107. **Jumbles:** FACET HABIT EXPEND VENDOR
Answer: Another name for a medical partnership—A PARADOX

108. **Jumbles:** ROACH SUITE HANDED FIXING
Answer: What the unemployed burlesque dancer had—NO "ACTS" TO GRIND

109. **Jumbles:** BRASS PRINT ENGULF KISMET
Answer: What the shrink's nervous patient was—"SELF-TAUT"

110. **Jumbles:** UPPER DINER STODGY FITFUL
Answer: She knows how to get more out of a dress than this—SHE PUTS INTO IT

111. **Jumbles:** FLUTE KITTY PLOVER FAMOUS
Answer: The cops were at the crooks' barbecue for this—A "STEAK OUT"

112. **Jumbles:** ANNOY WIPED TALLOW JOCKEY
Answer: The most common answer in the class—"I DON'T KNOW"

113. **Jumbles:** JUICE FRUIT UNLOAD JACKAL
Answer: That crazy magician seemed to lack this—A FULL DECK

114. **Jumbles:** CROON CYCLE FECUND DAHLIA
Answer: How the French sometimes conduct loan negotiations—"FRANC-LY"

115. **Jumbles:** BATHE POWER VALUED APPALL
Answer: What was the story about Moby Dick?—A WHALE TALE

116. **Jumbles:** COACH KEYED FUTURE FRIEZE
Answer: How the trainer reacted to the broken stopwatch—HE WAS "TICKED OFF"

117. **Jumbles:** FISHY WIPED SECOND HECKLE
Answer: A tactful husband always remembers his wife's birthday but forgets this—WHICH ONE IT IS

118. **Jumbles:** ANKLE YODEL DEADLY EITHER
Answer: What a criminal who falls into cement has to be—A HARDENED ONE

119. **Jumbles:** AUDIT NEWLY RAVAGE TRICKY
Answer: Whom to call if you're planning to give a banquet for your cat—THE "CAT-ERER"

120. **Jumbles:** NOISY SNORT BLUISH HEAVEN
Answer: What the lionesses might be—"NOISELESS"

121. **Jumbles:** AGLOW DIRTY FLIMSY COUGAR
Answer: What the percussion player enjoyed with his dinner—DRUM "ROLLS"

122. **Jumbles:** METAL REBEL MAYHEM ANSWER
Answer: What the oil tycoon said when asked to talk about the source of his wealth—IT'S BENEATH ME!

123. **Jumbles:** SLANT VIGIL THWART STUPID
Answer: What they said about the ghost—THAT'S THE SPIRIT!

124. **Jumbles:** GUILE CROAK INNING PSYCHE
Answer: Could be a roundabout way of showing your love—A HUG

125. **Jumbles:** BANAL EMBER VACUUM THROAT
Answer: What they called that guy who wouldn't lend any money—UNTOUCHABLE

126. **Jumbles:** FILMY PLAID FLORID PEOPLE
Answer: What the angry mummy did—FLIPPED HIS LID

127. **Jumbles:** GAMUT BULLY POCKET JOYFUL
Answer: How the anesthesiologist's patient felt—VERY "PUT OUT"

128. **Jumbles:** FAULT BLESS ATTACH EVOLVE
Answer: Why you might consult a plastic surgeon—TO SAVE FACE

129. **Jumbles:** MINUS EAGLE UNCOIL JOBBER
Answer: How the cotton tycoon found his work—VERY ABSORBING

130. **Jumbles:** LIVEN BROIL TINGLE MARROW
Answer: How the poor fish got hooked—WITH HIS OWN LINE

131. **Jumbles:** SKUNK BUILT SPONGE AUTUMN
Answer: They said the bachelor was never this—"MISS TAKEN"

132. **Jumbles:** LINEN AHEAD BIGAMY CLOVER
Answer: What she said to herself when the cardplayer proposed marriage—"NO BIG DEAL"

133. **Jumbles:** AWFUL SQUAW MALADY JAILED
Answer: What there seemed to be in that noisy courtroom—MORE "JAW" THAN LAW

134. **Jumbles:** GOURD HIKER ALBINO BELLOW
Answer: What they said about that evening gown—"LOW! — & BEHOLD"

135. **Jumbles:** LEAFY FOUNT LAWYER STOLID
Answer: What the geologist who specialized in earthquakes was—A "FAULT" FINDER

136. **Jumbles:** FINAL GAUDY EITHER CAUCUS
Answer: The only thing a pessimist ever expects on a silver platter—TARNISH

137. **Jumbles:** TONIC MOURN PULPIT BEACON
Answer: He became man of the hour because he knew how to make this—EVERY MINUTE COUNT

138. **Jumbles:** AGONY WEARY INHALE KINDLY
Answer: The bore wouldn't stop talking until his friend started this—WALKING

139. **Jumbles:** ICING AHEAD IMPACT CLOVER
Answer: Charged with something shocking—ELECTRIC

140. **Jumbles:** LOWLY TRILL NETHER INDUCT
Answer: A scratch pad is for people who have this at odd times and places—THE ITCH TO WRITE

141. **Jumbles:** FIFTY TAKEN GAINED ROBBER
Answer: What that deafening noise was a form of—"EAR-ITATION"

142. **Jumbles:** DRAFT JUMBO JUNKET HELMET
Answer: What a dog house is—A MUTT HUT

143. **Jumbles:** GAVEL FLANK SECOND MORBID
Answer: What the bouncer at the country and western club was—A FOLK "SLINGER"

144. **Jumbles:** FLUKE RODEO FITFUL DABBLE
Answer: What coffee often is—A "BREAK" FLUID

145. **Jumbles:** IGLOO CHAMP BALLET HYBRID
Answer: What New Year's Eve might be for some people—AN "ALCOHOLIDAY"

146. **Jumbles:** GAILY CAPON DAMASK HYMNAL
Answer: A girl with horse sense knows when to do this—SAY "NAY"

147. **Jumbles:** PLUME ABHOR BUOYED DURESS
Answer: What that dude became after marriage—SUBDUED

148. **Jumbles:** GUILT ABOVE WORTHY RITUAL
Answer: What does a small inlay cost these days?—A BIG OUTLAY

149. **Jumbles:** FISHY GOUGE SUGARY BELFRY
Answer: Figures don't lie—but liars to this—FIGURE

150. **Jumbles:** POUCH FORTY EXHALE CELERY
Answer: What that skillful witch was—A "HEX-PERT"

151. **Jumbles:** ELOPE AXIOM KOWTOW CLERGY
Answer: What the embarrassed Scotsman had—A "KILT" COMPLEX

152. **Jumbles:** FIFTY SQUAW TROUGH DEMISE
Answer: What tantrums in childhood appear to be—QUITE THE "RAGE"

153. **Jumbles:** JUICY MOUNT SUBURB CARPET
Answer: What did they give Dracula when he first went to Hollywood?—"BIT" PARTS

154. **Jumbles:** HOBBY PILOT PAYING FLATLY
Answer: What's a ball hit high in the air during a game played after dark?—A FLY-BY-NIGHT

155. **Jumbles:** TEASE ABOVE PREFER LUNACY
Answer: What some wrestling is a form of—BRUTE "FARCE"

156. **Jumbles:** HUMID TAKEN ENTICE CAUCUS
Answer: A guy who leaves too much to chance usually hasn't got this—A CHANCE

157. **Jumbles:** SNACK ELITE ORPHAN BELLOW
Answer: Success in life often depends on backbone, not this—WISHBONE

158. **Jumbles:** TONIC BOGUS TROPHY SMUDGE
Answer: What most vacationers seem to be these days—"MO-TOUR-ISTS"

159. **Jumbles:** GUILE AFTER SUBDUE GIGGLE
Answer: How she improved her knowledge—BY DEGREES

160. **Jumbles:** MAIZE GLORY TOUCHY WALRUS
Answer: What the octopus wore to the formal party—A COAT OF ARMS

161. **Jumbles:** FLORAL SHRIMP UPTOWN BEMUSE CLAMOR REVIVE
Answer: After losing his cool during a performance, Mozart needed to do this—COMPOSE HIMSELF

162. **Jumbles:** SMOGGY IGUANA PEOPLE CHROME HAMPER UNPACK
Answer: When they visited the capital of Italy, they had—"ROME-ING" CHARGES

163. **Jumbles:** CREAMY SHRINK RODENT IMPAIR SQUARE ODDEST
Answer: The magician didn't answer because he didn't like these—TRICK QUESTIONS

164. **Jumbles:** REMOVE INFUSE PEBBLE SAVORY UNFAIR SANDAL
Answer: When the AFC and NFC met in the championship game, everyone has a—SUPER SUNDAY

165. **Jumbles:** CRUTCH BESTOW FABRIC TROPHY PENCIL FALTER
Answer: Yogi and Boo Boo got into an accident on the runway due to faulty—"BEAR" TRAFFIC CONTROL

166. **Jumbles:** HAMPER UNWISE POCKET MOSTLY LATELY FLAVOR
Answer: When it came to the gemstones dating back to the days of pirates, he would—TREASURE THEM

167. **Jumbles:** PUBLIC ASYLUM PULLEY SHAKEN JERSEY OPAQUE
Answer: If felines built cars, their factories could feature these—ASSEMBLY "LIONS"

168. **Jumbles:** SICKEN YELLOW GENTLE JOYFUL GUTTER HECKLE
Answer: The Cyclopes weren't—SEEING EYE TO EYE

169. **Jumbles:** SKIMPY SWIVEL SAFARI FINALE UNLESS ENROLL
Answer: The hiking trail had this on it—ALL WALKS OF LIFE

170. **Jumbles:** FOSSIL AWAKEN GATHER PEANUT LEVITY WEEKLY
Answer: Renting the apartment was this for the zombie—A NEW LEASE ON LIFE

171. **Jumbles:** SUDDEN BUCKET PACKET PACIFY REMOVE LETTER
Answer: Of all the gifts you gave your mom on Mother's day, her favorite has always been—YOUR PRESENCE

172. **Jumbles:** SALUTE ETHNIC EMBODY FREELY SAVIOR OXYGEN
Answer: The comedian at the Death Valley comedy festival had a—DRY SENSE OF HUMOR

173. **Jumbles:** DETECT VIOLIN SANDAL EFFECT AUTHOR EMBLEM
Answer: The winner of the Indianapolis 500 was this—DRIVEN TO SUCCEED

174. **Jumbles:** ENOUGH MARKET INTACT INJURY SQUAWK DIVINE
Answer: He entered the bowling tournament in the hope of—STRIKING IT RICH

175. **Jumbles:** AFRAID DEFACE STENCH EXHALE SMOOTH DELUXE
Answer: After building a new deck underneath the large oak tree, he had it—MADE IN THE SHADE

176. **Jumbles:** PEOPLE ORIGIN EXCESS BATTEN SHRIMP ACIDIC
Answer: She wasn't surprised when her labor pains began because she was—EXPECTING THEM

177. **Jumbles:** THOUGH WEAPON UNTOLD SPIRAL OFFEND PANTRY
Answer: When the explorers reached the North Pole, they were—ON TOP OF THE WORLD

178. **Jumbles:** INSIST TRUANT PAUSED CANNON REGRET OUTAGE
Answer: The airport's security canine was the—"SCENTER" OF ATTENTION

179. **Jumbles:** FRUGAL SECEDE SNAPPY INHALE CHROME ATTAIN
Answer: The golfers caddie was—CALLING THE SHOTS

180. **Jumbles:** EXOTIC EMBARK SAILOR FLINCH JUNKET POETIC
Answer: After his new $100,000 sports car was in a collision, he was—BENT OUT OF SHAPE

Need More Jumbles®?

Jumble® Books

More than 175 puzzles each!

Cowboy Jumble®
• ISBN: 978-1-62937-355-3

Jammin' Jumble®
• ISBN: 978-1-57243-844-6

Java Jumble®
• ISBN: 978-1-60078-415-6

Jet Set Jumble®
• ISBN: 978-1-60078-353-1

Jolly Jumble®
• ISBN: 978-1-60078-214-5

Jumble® Anniversary
• ISBN: 987-1-62937-734-6

Jumble® Ballet
• ISBN: 978-1-62937-616-5

Jumble® Birthday
• ISBN: 978-1-62937-652-3

Jumble® Celebration
• ISBN: 978-1-60078-134-6

Jumble® Champion
• ISBN: 978-1-62937-870-1

Jumble® Coronation
• ISBN: 978-1-62937-976-0

Jumble® Cuisine
• ISBN: 978-1-62937-735-3

Jumble® Drag Race
• ISBN: 978-1-62937-483-3

Jumble® Ever After
• ISBN: 978-1-62937-785-8

Jumble® Explorer
• ISBN: 978-1-60078-854-3

Jumble® Explosion
• ISBN: 978-1-60078-078-3

Jumble® Fever
• ISBN: 978-1-57243-593-3

Jumble® Galaxy
• ISBN: 978-1-60078-583-2

Jumble® Garden
• ISBN: 978-1-62937-653-0

Jumble® Genius
• ISBN: 978-1-57243-896-5

Jumble® Geography
• ISBN: 978-1-62937-615-8

Jumble® Getaway
• ISBN: 978-1-60078-547-4

Jumble® Gold
• ISBN: 978-1-62937-354-6

Jumble® Health
• ISBN: 978-1-63727-085-1

Jumble® Jackpot
• ISBN: 978-1-57243-897-2

Jumble® Jailbreak
• ISBN: 978-1-62937-002-6

Jumble® Jambalaya
• ISBN: 978-1-60078-294-7

Jumble® Jitterbug
• ISBN: 978-1-60078-584-9

Jumble® Journey
• ISBN: 978-1-62937-549-6

Jumble® Jubilation
• ISBN: 978-1-62937-784-1

Jumble® Jubilee
• ISBN: 978-1-57243-231-4

Jumble® Juggernaut
• ISBN: 978-1-60078-026-4

Jumble® Kingdom
• ISBN: 978-1-62937-079-8

Jumble® Knockout
• ISBN: 978-1-62937-078-1

Jumble® Madness
• ISBN: 978-1-892049-24-7

Jumble® Magic
• ISBN: 978-1-60078-795-9

Jumble® Mania
• ISBN: 978-1-57243-697-8

Jumble® Marathon
• ISBN: 978-1-60078-944-1

Jumble® Masterpiece
• ISBN: 978-1-62937-916-6

Jumble® Neighbor
• ISBN: 978-1-62937-845-9

Jumble® Parachute
• ISBN: 978-1-62937-548-9

Jumble® Party
• ISBN: 978-1-63727-008-0

Jumble® Safari
• ISBN: 978-1-60078-675-4

Jumble® Sensation
• ISBN: 978-1-60078-548-1

Jumble® Skyscraper
• ISBN: 978-1-62937-869-5

Jumble® Symphony
• ISBN: 978-1-62937-131-3

Jumble® Theater
• ISBN: 978-1-62937-484-0

Jumble® Time Machine: 1972
• ISBN: 978-1-63727-082-0

Jumble® Trouble
• ISBN: 978-1-62937-917-3

Jumble® University
• ISBN: 978-1-62937-001-9

Jumble® Unleashed
• ISBN: 978-1-62937-844-2

Jumble® Vacation
• ISBN: 978-1-60078-796-6

Jumble® Wedding
• ISBN: 978-1-62937-307-2

Jumble® Workout
• ISBN: 978-1-60078-943-4

Jump, Jive and Jumble®
• ISBN: 978-1-60078-215-2

Lunar Jumble®
• ISBN: 978-1-60078-853-6

Monster Jumble®
• ISBN: 978-1-62937-213-6

Mystic Jumble®
• ISBN: 978-1-62937-130-6

Rainy Day Jumble®
• ISBN: 978-1-60078-352-4

Royal Jumble®
• ISBN: 978-1-60078-738-6

Sports Jumble®
• ISBN: 978-1-57243-113-3

Summer Fun Jumble®
• ISBN: 978-1-57243-114-0

Touchdown Jumble®
• ISBN: 978-1-62937-212-9

Oversize Jumble® Books

More than 500 puzzles!

Colossal Jumble®
• ISBN: 978-1-57243-490-5

Jumbo Jumble®
• ISBN: 978-1-57243-314-4

Jumble® Crosswords™

More than 175 puzzles!

Jumble® Crosswords™
• ISBN: 978-1-57243-347-2

NFL DRAFT ELITE 60

THE 2016 SUPERSTARS OF TOMORROW

DANE BRUGLER

TRIUMPH
BOOKS

This book is available in quantity at special discounts for your group or organization.

For further information, contact:

Triumph Books LLC
814 N. Franklin
Chicago, Illinois 60610
www.triumphbooks.com

Printed in United States of America
ISBN: 978-1-62937-274-7
Design by Andy Hansen
Editorial and page production by Alex Lubertozzi
Photos courtesy of AP Images unless otherwise indicated